POEMS IN THE CASE

POEMS IN THE CASE

MICHAEL BARTHOLOMEW-BIGGS

All rights reserved. No part of this work covered by the copyright herein may be reproduced or used in any means – graphic, electronic, or mechanical, including copying, recording, taping, or information storage and retrieval systems – without written permission of the publisher.

Printed by imprintdigital
Upton Pyne, Exeter
www.digital.imprint.co.uk

Typesetting and cover design by narrator
www.narrator.me.uk
info@narrator.me.uk
033 022 300 39

Published by Shoestring Press
19 Devonshire Avenue, Beeston, Nottingham, NG9 1BS
(0115) 925 1827
www.shoestringpress.co.uk

First published 2018
© Copyright: Michael Bartholomew-Biggs
© Cover photograph by Florian Klauer on Unsplash

The moral right of the author has been asserted.

ISBN 978-1-912524-05-1

ABOUT THE AUTHOR

Michael Bartholomew-Biggs is a semi-retired mathematician who still functions as poetry editor of the on-line magazine *London Grip* and co-organiser of the North London reading series *Poetry in the Crypt*. His most recent publications are *Fred & Blossom* (Shoestring Press, 2013), *Pictures from a Postponed Exhibition* (Lapwing, 2014) and *The Man Who Wasn't Ever Here* (Wayleave, 2017). More about his life and times can be found at http://mikeb-b.blogspot.com/

ACKNOWLEDGEMENTS

The author is grateful to the editors and publishers of the following magazines, anthologies and collections in which (versions of) some of the poems in this book have previously appeared: *Acumen, Ambit, The Bow-Wow Shop, Brittle Star, Clear Poetry, The Coffee House, Dreamcatcher, The Editor—a festschrift for Patricia Oxley* (Rockingham Press, 2011), *Envoi, Frogmore Papers, From the City to the Saltings* (Essex Poetry Festival anthology 2013), *The High Window, Inklings of Complicity* (Pikestaff Press, 2003), *Ink Sweat & Tears, The Interpreter's House, Iota, KG Confidential—a festschrift for Katherine Gallagher* (Circle Time Press, 2015), *The Lampeter Review, London Grip, Message in a Bottle, morphrog, Obsessed with Pipework, Orbis, Orni-thology* (Poetry Wivenhoe, 2016), *Other Poetry, Penniless Press, The Salon of the Refused, Seam, The SHOp, Smiths Knoll, South, South Bank Poetry, The Spectator, The Stare's Nest, Truths; A Telltale Anthology* (Telltale Press, 2018), *Under the Radar, Uneasy Relations* (Hearing Eye, 2007).

Particular thanks are also due to Don Atkinson, Nancy Mattson, James Norcliffe and Paul Richards who all made very helpful suggestions during the development of this book. Individual poems have benefited from workshop discussions with many poetry friends—especially Fawzia Kane, Martin Noutch, Anna Robinson, John Roe and Katherine Venn.

FOREWORD

This collection is certainly not the first to place poems inside a prose narrative. Nor is it the first narrative to be set in a residential poetry workshop. Vernon Scannell's *Feminine Endings* (Enitharmon 2000) makes use of such a location with all its potential for conflicts and liaisons between the participants.

In Scannell's book however matters do not get as far as murder. Hence, when I began writing *Poems in the Case*, I hoped I was breaking new ground by placing poems within the framework of a detective story. But it turns out that I was over-optimistic. As I was completing my final draft I came across a copy of *Death Comes for the Poets* (Muswell Press 2012) by Matthew Sweeney and John Hartley Williams. This is a fast moving whodunit in which about thirteen eminent poets are murdered. Both the investigator and perpetrator are poets too. The various victims are done to death in dramatic ways that match themes in their most famous poems. In one of the less gory killings, a poet who often uses drowning as a metaphor is despatched by being tipped into the sea from the Fishguard ferry.

Although *Poems in the Case* is a shorter narrative than *Death Comes for the Poets* and has a much lower body count both books belong to a genre of which Messrs Sweeney & Hartley Williams have a prior claim to be the inventors.

CONTENTS

PROLOGUE: DEATH OF A POET	1
Sharp Objects	3
EPISODE 1: A SURPRISE ANNOUNCEMENT & A PROFESSIONAL RIVALRY	4
National Trust	6
Arrangement for Strings	7
EPISODE 2: APPLICATIONS FOR A POETRY WORKSHOP	8
Digital Alarm 1999	10
Child's Play	11
Criminal Tendencies	12
Labyrinth	13
Famous Father	14
Courtship Dance	15
EPISODE 3: POETS ASSEMBLE ON A SUNDAY AFTERNOON	16
EPISODE 4: POETS BEGIN TO REVEAL THEMSELVES	19
Extra Passenger	21
Process of Elimination	22
Nothing Outward	24
Unsafe House	25
Windsurfer	27
Intourist—Иностранный Турист	29
EPISODE 5: CONFLICTS & SURPRISES ON MONDAY	31
Quality Time	34
Grand Mal	35
Medical History	37
Moving Violation	38
Pharmaceuticals	39
Sincerest Form	41

EPISODE 6: SETBACKS & TENSIONS ON TUESDAY	44
Memoirs of a Fxxx-Hunting Man	46
&	47
Primary Colouring	48
All of Me	49
Rhyme, Regret & Irrational Optimism in Canadian Country & Western Lyrics	50
In San Gimignano	52
EPISODE 7: PROVOCATIONS & REACTIONS ON WEDNESDAY	54
The Fox-Hunting Ban	56
Sewage & Money—Spot the Difference	57
A Financier Resists the Statutory Minimum Wage	58
Branding	59
EPISODE 8: A TIMELY DISTRACTION	60
Re-Reading Nineteen Eighty-Four	61
EPISODE 9: SHOCKING DISCOVERIES ON THURSDAY	64
Don't Try This at Home	68
EPISODE 10: STANLEY READS A LETTER	69
EPISODE 11: A QUESTION OF DATES	73
Emotional Trajectories	73
EPISODE 12: AN INCONSISTENCY AND ITS CONSEQUENCES	75
EPISODE 13: A CARELESS MISTAKE	79
EPISODE 14: A RESOLUTION?	82
Before I Proved the Theorem …	84
EPISODE 15: AND AFTERWARDS…	85

AN IMAGE ON THE RETINA	89
End of Holiday	91
Same Time Some Other Year	92
Slow Turns of Events (1)	94
Ascending	95
Simmer Gently	96
En Suite	97
Warning off	98
Slow Turns of Events (2)	99
Maybe Not	100
Two Minutes' Silence	101
Mourners	102
Feeling the Cold	103
Adagio	104
Slow Turns of Events (3)	105
Urban Concealment	106
Free Running	108
Street Theatre	109
Sick in a Strange City	110
Slow Turns of Events (4)	113
Dawn Solo	114
Double Entry	115
When the Photograph Was Taken	117
An Image on the Retina	118

Prologue: Death of a poet

On 17 April 1995, the body of the poet Eric Jessop was recovered from rocks below the cliffs at Bogburgh in Devon, near the cottage he shared with his partner and fellow-poet George Hamblin. It was Hamblin who reported discovering the body soon after his return from leading a poetry workshop in Sussex. A post-mortem revealed that Jessop had been dead about eighteen hours. His body showed only abrasions consistent with a fall, so the eventual verdict of suicide came as no surprise—especially in view of Hamblin's evidence that his partner had been depressed for several months. *Eric's writing wasn't going well—in fact we were a dismal pair because I'd been taking on so many workshops that my poetry was suffering too.... I wish now I hadn't left poor Eric alone for that whole week.*

During the police investigation which followed the tragedy, the hard disk on Jessop's computer was found to have been wiped clean—perhaps as a last despairing gesture. A couple of handwritten poem fragments on his desk were the only evidence of recent composition.

> I shared his strange affection for O'Brien
> who understood how little is surrendered
> by ~~admitting~~ confessing to rebellion below the waist.
> but I can only guess ~~how fiercely you resent~~
>   your fierce resentment

of the state ~~we're in~~ we've reached—
both cheated by my own O'Brien
who after all and all the time has been in charge

>The bull ~~buckles~~ collapses,
>forelegs ~~folding~~ buckling
>at the second poleaxe blow.
>Eyeballs freeze and hold/fix
>two cameo reflections
>of the ~~butcher~~ slaughterman, bare-lit
>beside a smeared and spattered wall.

Jessop was in his early thirties when he died, but he had already published four well-received collections. He was a popular figure at festivals and readings thanks to his easy charm, which managed to be both larger-than-life and also self-deprecating. His career is well summarised in this tribute from a major poetry journal.

Eric Jessop, born in Wales in 1961, was the only child of a teacher and a parish priest. Both his parents died in a plane crash during his first year at university in London. After this tragedy he suspended his studies for a year, during which he began writing and publishing the powerful poems that formed the basis of his debut collection, Which Way To Turn. *This won the Appledore Prize in 1985. In Jessop's later books*—The Site of Blood *(1987),* The Code for Apricots *(1990) and* Cognitive Perspective *(1993)—the rawness of his early work gradually gave way to a more objective and quizzical tone. Jessop always acknowledged a huge debt to his poetic mentor George Hamblin who was writer-in-residence during Jessop's final university year. Other influences include Philip Larkin "who made poems from the bleakly ordinary"; Stevie Smith "always utterly herself"; and, surprisingly, Leonard Cohen "the contemporary voice of an Old Testament prophet".*

The last of Jessop's poems to appear during his lifetime was featured in a high-profile (but perhaps rather pretentious) anthology from Oxblood Books entitled *The Beginning of the End—poems from the first half of a century's closing decade.* With hindsight, it could be said to reveal some possibly self-destructive anxieties...

SHARP OBJECTS

A slim serrated blade of panic
penetrates your rind and bacon body
as the bookshop café table tilts
beneath your elbow and your plate
and lunch and cappuccino
are about to slide and smash
in front of all these well-bred readers.

You gasp and grasp but nothing's moving
only you and this small moment
has not started a calamity.
Yet some calamities are started
by one lurch of failure. When a corkscrew,
exiting a cork askew, impales
a thumb, the bottle falls and breaks.

Once a skewer of alarm goes in
the flesh beneath your shirt gets seasoned
with salt and pepper specks of sweat.
Imagined rows of razor gazes
shave away the blushing layers
of your nerve-rich epidermis
into ragged flakes like Parmesan.

Episode 1: A surprise announcement & a professional rivalry

In early 1999, almost four years after Eric Jessop's death, Epidermis Press (*Writing to get under the skin*) caused a mild stir by announcing the forthcoming publication of a collection of previously unseen Jessop poems. Epidermis had brought out all Jessop's previous books (including a hastily compiled *Collected Poems* soon after his death). The publisher, Stephen Prince, when asked why this work had not appeared sooner, spoke only of *wanting to distance it from the circumstances of Eric's death*. George Hamblin, when pressed for his opinion, conjectured that Prince must be planning to publish some of Eric's very early work since his last months had been extremely unproductive. Hamblin's lack of enthusiasm about Prince's publishing *coup* was of course understandable since it would inevitably stir up painful memories for him.

After Eric's death, Hamblin had sold the Devon cottage and moved to Exeter where he lived alone and eventually resumed reviewing, tutoring and composing the well-made poems of reminiscence for which he was widely admired. He was known to be a contender for the prestigious and lucrative post of poet-in-residence at the investment company McMahon

Associates (often pronounced "Mammon"). Unfortunately, his rival for the position was none other than Stephen Prince who, besides being a publisher, was also a poet, specialising in dark, enigmatic narratives. Hamblin could therefore be forgiven for worrying that the publicity surrounding the new Jessop book would give Prince a decisive advantage.

Opinions among the members of the McMahon selection panel were, in fact, sharply divided. Some thought Hamblin's cosily nostalgic verses carried reassuring implications of investor security while others felt that Prince's darker, edgier poems suggested positive ideas of enterprise and profitable risk-taking. Their contrasting styles can be seen in two examples presented to the McMahon Associates Cultural Capital (Poetry) Panel (currently adjourned *sine die*)...

NATIONAL TRUST
by George Hamblin

I cut along the Cromwell Road towards Ham House.
A mistress of intrigue lived here in Cromwell's time;
and all the staff have fallen half in love with Lady Dysart,
Restoration Mata Hari.

The Kingston bypass keeps its promise, points me on to Selborne,
in whose car park Rovers will be over-represented.
(But for me to mention that might be a touch
too much like Betjeman.)

I'm out to mix with other, older English icons:
Gilbert White, meticulous in documenting downland flowers
(never *eidelweiss* or *pis-en-lit*);

and Turner, making permanent a moment's movement, fixing it
in Petworth light, diffused as if by wind-snatched ashes
scattering across the sun.

I would once have drawn a line at fancying a cup of tea
and slice of sponge to follow galleries of portraits
and someone else's limed-oak furniture.

But by the time I get to Uppark I'll be feeling
like the aging peer who married his best dairymaid,
attracted—as King David was to Abishag—
by a pair of firm, warm, trusted hands.

The National Trust properties in this poem form a straightish line between London and the south coast. Events such as Sir Harry Fetherstonhaugh's late marriage at Uppark House are drawn from National Trust websites.

ARRANGEMENT FOR STRINGS
by Stephen Prince

Jazz and puppetry, she says
are twins. She's right: harmonic lines
allow as little freedom
as a finger up the spine
or wires through wrists that push or pull you
into false positions.

> I'm a home-made marionette.
> She holds the strings. *Come here*, she calls,
> pretending that she doesn't;
> next she'll brush me with a kiss
> or with a lash. I won't ask which
> until I close the door.

>> Should she cut me loose I'd slump,
>> a bundle of discordant limbs.
>> Puppetry and jazz
>> run risks: alfresco melodies
>> divorced from chords collapse, go sprawling
>> as disjointed notes.

> She's making me negotiate
> departures: clean out china/filing
> cabinets and clear
> the desktop/bedside diary;
> leave notelets for my next/my old
> employer/landlord/lover.

Puppetry works hand in glove
with jazz. My first-choice orchestra
has been marched away
in chains and handcuffs; in its place
a second string quintet rehearses
ersatz hot club music.

Episode 2: Applications for a poetry workshop

The McMahon selectors had not yet made a decision when, in April 1999, George Hamblin and Stephen Prince were booked to lead a week-long poetry workshop at Weald Barn writer's centre in Kent. The workshop title—"Delighting in the Dark Side"—had initially been proposed by Prince to reflect his own poetic style; but the pairing with Hamblin was suggested by the Weald Barn administrator Julia Nelson. Julia had run the centre very successfully for a couple of years; and, although not herself a writer, she was the kind of efficient manager that "creatives" need but rarely value. She had been tempted by the piquancy of asking the two McMahon rivals to work together and was pleased when news broke about the pending Jessop collection since this would surely generate even more interest in the workshop.

Weald Barn was an unusually small establishment, partly supported by a legacy from a literary-minded manufacturer of tomato sauce. Converted from a group of oast houses, it had room for only eight visitors. Its high fees were justified by the excellent tutor-tutee ratio and also by the quality of meals supplied by an outside catering firm—much better than the do-it-yourself cooking arrangements at most other residential workshops. In the circumstances, the number of applications for "Delighting in the Dark Side" easily exceeded Weald Barn's capacity. Hence Julia and the two tutors chose six tutees (or "guests" in Weald Barn parlance) on the basis of their submission of a small batch of poems.

Some initial impressions of these guests may be gained from a sample of the poems which accompanied their applications and are still in the Weald Barn archives.

DIGITAL ALARM 1999
by Stanley Spenser

If you thought this year's end meant emergencies
or supposed that rows of zeros were important
then you gave too much significance to fingers.

Octal anniversaries that might have been,
were the norm two less, have gone unmarked; two extra
and four figure years arrived while Dr Halley
hunted other comets in the Greenwich skies
and hummed unpublished firework tunes by Mr Handel.

CHILD'S PLAY
by Daisie Blake

This game's rules
scarcely need elaboration:
they'll be forgotten
by both participants and lunchtime.
The pleasure is
to spell out loud the solid facts
of fantasy:
the time the shop is going to open;
the special chairs
where the customers must sit
to have their fittings;
the yellow of that unseen door
whose silent bell
gains entry to an empty stockroom
from which to fetch out
silver slippers on a coffee tray.

CRIMINAL TENDENCIES
by Barry Wigfall

I was talking in my sleep to this policeman.
What it is, he said, is this. You trust your judgement.
You get real close in up against your suspect
then you lean on him
(and here he rubbed his face on mine)
and you notice his reaction.
You can always tell the guilty ones.

Does it stand up well in court? He didn't answer
but applied his cheek again and I could feel
reactions that were asking to be noticed.

But what I want to know, I said,
is how many of the people
get to pass your test and walk away?
None of them, he smiled, and that's the point.
That's the way we know we've got it right.

LABYRINTH
by Abigail Forsberg

He came up from the south
                      a tad off- course already
but *nothing you need fuss about*, he told himself, *you're close enough*.
And even as he sensed a further drift   *away*
and not *toward* he wasn't much alarmed.

It took an actual obstacle(
But was it really there? Or something he'd made up?
) to make him double back
                      and
look for ways around it.

The going got much smoother then and one more easy zig-
    zag promised steady progress with his goal in constant view—
        though some way to the right, the distance not diminishing.

He reckoned he had found a way back by a back way
to the centre when his near-tangential track
                          turned
             inward
twice.
He'd barely ever been so close; and never for so long.

But even that was not the end of it; he stumbled out
                      & out again
                          to trudge
                              a weary half-
                          circumference,
                    not seeing
lowest points as opportunities for rising to occasions.

FAMOUS FATHER
by Mary Maxwell

When the garden doors were his
They opened wide to lawns and adulation:
Now his daughter keeps them closed
And mildewed glass rough-mirrors unmown grass.
A roller stands amid admiring daisies.

He used to welcome weekend guests from London:
Imitators, rivals, famous faces
He had painted, others he still hoped to,
Editors commissioning more illustrations
For *The Listener* or *Radio Times*.

The daisies sway, untroubled
That a quarter of them could be crushed
When the roller moves again.
Since his funeral, she's left the lawns
Unsmoothed, subsiding into meadowness.

Overgrowth surrounds the under-cared-for house
Whose off-white wash is worn like last night's makeup.
Window-corner paint has cracked to crow's feet.
Callers tut at rusted gutters,
Drooping like two puffy eyelids.

The studio survives.
She works there using fabric, dyes and wire—
Less male and academic tools
Than brush and pen that made her father's name
A name some visitors still recognize.

The bolder ones who ask "Are you related…?"
Scan her gallery again with altered eyes:
And if she sees straight lips mime "H'm, not quite"
She always hears his photograph agree
"Yes, more like something from an evening craft class."

COURTSHIP DANCE
by Frederick Willoughby

Sometimes it's just a turning of the head
to look along a certain street;
or else the small diversion past
the house itself. Is her car outside?
He knows other places that are visited
and checks them intermittently,
reassured to see that nothing new
is happening. No need for jealousy
over gatherings of three or four.

No one sees him through those evening windows:
no one thinks to look. But might there be
an early morning glance, like his,
that scans the half-full office car park
to see who else is in?
                          At five o'clock
he likes to keep an eye on people leaving
with an open folder on his desk
for snapping shut and jumping up
in time to brush against her on the stairs.

Episode 3: Poets assemble on a Sunday afternoon

Stanley Spenser was very pleased to learn his application to attend "Delighting in the Dark Side" had been successful; he had already booked that week as part of his annual leave. (In the government department where he worked, holiday requests at short notice were regarded unfavourably.)

On the Sunday when the workshop was due to start, Stanley arrived at the railway station for Weald Barn a little earlier than the recommended hour. He reasoned he could fill the time either by walking the mile or so to his destination or by having a cup of tea in a café and then taking a taxi. He was still undecided which to do when he was approached by the only other passenger to get off the train. She was a smartly dressed woman of about sixty and Stanley thought her face looked familiar.

I'm willing to bet you and I are bound for the same place, she said in very clear RP tones. *I believe you are a poet who delights in the dark side and I claim my prize!*

Stanley was never comfortable with people who spoke in such flamboyant language. But it was simple enough for him to admit that he had been identified correctly and to introduce himself. In his slightly nervous state, however, he was unable to refrain from adding his habitual and redundant half-apology for being no relation to *the* Stanley Spencer.

And I'm Mary Maxwell, said his new companion. She decided not to remark that Stanley did in fact bear a marked resemblance to the famous artist with his combed-forward hair and round rimless glasses.

Stanley now knew why her face was familiar. She was a moderately successful character actor who had been in a number of long-running television series.

Well, let's grab a taxi and get going, she said.

Stanley pointed out that they were, strictly speaking, not supposed to arrive at Weald Barn for another twenty minutes. Mary was splendidly dismissive of this observation: *Well, what are they going to do—pour boiling oil on us? They're much more likely to smile and put the kettle on!*

During the short taxi ride Mary made quite sure that Stanley knew who she was by explaining how she had begun reading poetry—and subsequently writing it—to pass the time backstage *whenever I'm not on till Act Three or make my last exit in Act One*. In response Stanley felt obliged to mention his own day job as a mathematician—which was something else he tended to be apologetic about since people often seemed to find it threatening. He gave no details about his work in a high-security government department for communications and encryption.

Stanley and Mary were indeed the first—and slightly early—arrivals, but Mary's optimistic forecast about the welcome at Weald Barn proved correct. Julia, the administrator, greeted them warmly and showed them into the lounge where tea and cakes were served almost immediately.

Within the next hour or so, all the other guests arrived, some by car and some on the next train. The afternoon went by in a flurry of introductions, half-finished conversations and attempts to share and absorb names and a few personal details. Stanley was more of a watcher and listener than a talker and probably did as well as anyone at retaining an initial impression of each of the guests.

Daisie Blake arrived only a few minutes after Stanley and Mary had poured their first cups of tea. She was in her mid-forties, pretty in a fluffy sort of way but with sad blue eyes. She was soon followed by Frederick Willoughby. He was a heavily built man, nearing sixty, who had a permanently down-turned mouth. He was wearing—as it turned out he almost always did—a musty-smelling tweed jacket.

The next to appear was the much more eye-catching Abigail Forsberg (*you say it "Force-berry"*). She was a tall and strikingly beautiful twenty-something Canadian postgraduate student with a fondness for brightly-coloured scarves. Abigail was accompanied by Barry Wigfall who had evidently met her on the train. He was also in his twenties and had a long mischievous face. He already had a PhD and a job with a major publisher. In a pleasant Yorkshire accent he suggested that people might like to *call me Baz*, but few of the other guests took him up on this.

The bio-note cliché *his/her poems have appeared in many magazines* was applicable to all six of the guests. The two youngest seemed already to have featured in a number of prestigious publications while Willoughby's most productive years appeared to be some way behind him. Daisie and Abigail were the only ones to have published a (small) collection.

Quite a varied bunch, Stanley said to himself. *I wonder how we'll all get along.*

Then another thought struck him. *I wonder how we'll get along with the tutors…?*

Episode 4: Poets begin to reveal themselves

It was customary at Weald Barn for the tutors not to join the guests until the Sunday evening meal, after which they could mingle in a "drinks-and-get-to-know-one-another" session. On this occasion the mingling did not go particularly well. Relations between Hamblin and Prince seemed strained and Julia began to wonder if it had been such a good idea to invite the two McMahon rivals as co-tutors. Daisie Blake embarrassed Prince by frequently reminding him of their previous meetings at festivals where his readings *had been the highlight*. Frederick Willoughby was also very attentive to Prince—but in a less admiring way, pestering him with questions about how many new authors Epidermis had taken on recently and pressing him to explain his approach to the assessment of unsolicited submissions. Mary Maxwell, by contrast, was charming to everyone—but with an intensity that could have been mistaken for over-acting. Stanley remained quiet and invisible enough for some of the others to feel a little guilty for not doing more to include him in conversation. Abigail and Barry, having sat together at supper, now seemed intent on becoming invisible to everybody but each other.

The two tutors sought to bring an unsatisfactory evening to a more successful conclusion by spending a few minutes explaining how the workshop would be divided into exercises, discussions and one-to-one tutorials. *I wouldn't like to claim George and I have over-organised proceedings,* Prince confessed. *But we did agree that tonight we'd both read a couple of poems to show how easily darkness can slip into an ordinary setting when things go just a tiny bit awry.* With what seemed like exaggerated politeness, Prince then stepped aside to let his fellow tutor speak.

Stanley, who had not seen Hamblin perform before, now observed that his height (well over six feet) gave him an imposing presence. He was around fifty and his well-built frame was running very slightly to fat while his cheeks were only a little pinker and puffier than in his back-cover photographs. He began with *something from a workshop exercise where the first line must include three random words drawn from a hat. Maybe we'll try that one tomorrow ...*

> *Severity is a feathery kitchen*
> *stocked with cutting edges, chopping boards*
> *unsoftened by the layers of downy fragments*
> *from this morning's little victims.*

This produced a few chuckles and mock-shudders from his audience. Hamblin then delivered two more poems which *I've put a bit more effort into. I think they show that threats can be most powerful when they creep into seemingly normal situations. And I do literally mean creep...*

EXTRA PASSENGER

The way you don't, I didn't
look at him, the pre-existing occupant
of the only partly-empty seat remaining on the bus.

You're brave he said—which made no sense
until I saw the plastic box, with thoughtful air holes, on his lap.
So what's in there? I asked, my voice maybe a quartertone too high
as I pretended to be keen on peering through
the box's scratched translucent sides, supposing he supposed
I'd shudder if I saw a scorpion's black scuttle
or striped coils of snake, an Orwell sewer rat—or worse

a mouse-sized tufted thing suspended
under far too many jointed legs. He smiled
It isn't in the box he said, holding out his hand towards me...

    I suppose I should call that a "found poem", said Hamblin with a smile,—*or perhaps even a pilfered one—since the incident actually happened to a friend of mine. The next one is entirely fantasy however* ... In a stage-whispered aside he added *All the same, I think it may strike a particular chord for you, Stephen.* Stanley assumed this must relate to some private joke.

PROCESS OF ELIMINATION

Eventually,
whenever I approached his door,
I began indulging in the hope
of finding him not there—
and, you understand,
not just not there:
not anywhere.

Rapture,
alien abduction,
spontaneous combustion,
or a fall down awkward stairs—
for none of these could I be blamed,
or blame myself. Surprise would be my alibi:
for as I willed his non-existence
I knew my will had never yet
(been proved to have)
accomplished much.

At his threshold
I'd focus on a middle ground
beyond the briar-patch of actualities
to where a fantasy might turn out to be true.
And there, in open fields, the clichés romped:
I'd have the "options" other people had;
to find him gone would let me
"find myself".

Small rehearsals
of his tidy disappearance were,
I often tell myself, a harmless way
of getting through the bad times
until it really happened.

Well, thank you for that sample of understated malice, George, said Prince as he took Hamblin's place at the lectern. *Let's see if I can match it.*

As a performer, Prince—notwithstanding Daisie Blake's excessive admiration—was less impressive than Hamblin, being some six inches shorter and possessing a thinner, more nasal voice. But he was trimly built and his dark hair was very lightly touched with grey in the manner that Italians approvingly call *brizzolato*. He started with a haiku called "Hostage Negotiation"

> *They'll only free me*
> *if I won't tell what they did*
> *to all the others.*

and then moved smoothly on to his more substantial pieces, which he performed back-to-back after a single—and frankly superfluous—introduction. *The first one gets inside the gloomy breakdown of a once close relationship; and after that we hear the futile optimism and self-distraction of someone in hiding who knows he is bound to be discovered.*

NOTHING OUTWARD

There was unease sulking in the bass line
the whole morning
while we were driving down through Worcestershire,
with reminders from the radio between us
of the issue that was pushing us apart.
Each lyric seemed contrived to make us draw
another inference of infidelity—
a fact which neither of us could admit
sufficiently to reach and turn it off.

Shame whined meanly in the treble clef,
in shrill insistence
that nothing outward had been untoward
and that it hadn't mattered when attraction
was hastily denied and then admitted.
But even if we said a glimpse of glances
had caught the full extent of indiscretion,
could we resolve all tension in the theme
of betrayal lying only with the flesh?

UNSAFE HOUSE

I wake up feeling bruised by dreams.
Last night was full of clattering—
a pebbledash of hail
on windows. Sashes rattle still.
My rituals with match and gas disturb a battered kettle

whose mumble-whispering resembles
soft wind thickened by fine rain.
Coffee keeps its promise
better than most manifestos:
after me, the sewer rats will get their caffeine rush.

The kitchen's contents disappoint:
my nose recoils from chlorine scents
of pears gone past their prime.
Tepid fruit-drink cartons boast
they're not from concentrate then split and spill juice on my hand

so when I slip the sugar pot's
white slotted lid around the spoon
my finger prints remain
as forensic evidence
suggesting I've been bleeding from an undiscovered wound.

I ought to blame the absent landlord
rather than the former tenants
for the choice of pictures.
Each portrait is an alias
and landscapes are all alibis no one should believe.

A moving target has to deal
with what's not happened yet. I trust
the telephone to bring
routine recorded messages
which say if I should be allowed, or be afraid to leave.

As Prince finished reading, Daisie commented loudly on *the clever half rhymes at the end of the stanzas* and a round of polite applause seemed to be bringing the evening to a close. But even as people were getting up from their seats Prince seemed struck by a sudden thought. *I'm going to spring something on George now*, he told the audience. *Since we'll both be critiquing your work all this week maybe we should be willing to expose our own poems to public analysis. So I'd like to read you one of George's poems and make a few comments on it—and then he can do the same for me. Is that OK with you George?*

Hamblin probably felt he had to make a gesture of assent. Prince went on. *For me, this poem brilliantly gets inside the head of someone on the dark border between taking responsibility and shirking it. In fact George also perfectly hit that note of pretend powerlessness in one he read just now—"Process of Elimination" wasn't it?*

WINDSURFER

Fast and upright
and exposed
he rides his private radius
towards a circle's unknown centre. Surf's
the safe circumference: but how will he get back?

He must be sick with indecision.
Tack back upwind? Make landfall on
an out-of-sight side of the bay? Or vanish
in mid-ocean? On a bolting horse you'd cling

until it dropped; or fall and hope
to walk home bruised. He either rides
untiring wind, or swims—which looks too far.
It's getting late. There's no one on the beach to wave to;

only me
high on this cliff,
mind clenched, imagining a plight
which might be quite imaginary—since he's
gone out on his own he surely knows what's what?

What I don't know is how to call
the coastguard and what locals call
this stretch of coast. So I suspect I'll act
as if I'd seen a suspect package on a bus:

ignore it; sidle off. My fear
of feeling burdened but inept
is strong enough to stand on, skimming over
any shallow inshore currents of concern.

Congratulations George, said Prince as he sat down again. *Do you want to try a quid pro quo? It doesn't have to be complimentary!*

Hamblin had been thumbing through a copy of Prince's latest collection while his own poem was being read and had evidently found something suitable. He announced the poem's title and its Russian equivalent (which he pronounced quite accurately, Stanley noticed) and then complimented Prince on *creating a threatening atmosphere and hinting at hidden secrets with nothing more than a spot of Cyrillic trickery. But what I think he's* really *doing is to lure his readers into colluding with him in a frothy fantasy with no mystery at all! We admire his rhetorical skill even when we know it's simply there to hide the lack of substance! Very clever!*

INTOURIST—ИНОСТРАННЫЙ ТУРИСТ

Nothing hides the fishbone rolls of razor wire
from tourists as the train grinds in beside the prison.
This—the city's oldest building—is still serving
its intended purpose. Post-war reconstruction
of the bombed hotel has kept the worn-down steps.
In its lobby, tilted mirrors ricochet
the guests' identities along bleak corridors.

And this is where I'm closing in on Lisi.
Is she at reception with dark-eyed Tamara?
Lisi always used to smile when I was late.
If I came in tired Tamara didn't care.

The hotel restaurant's been overhauled again
but still is overstaffed by grim-faced waitresses.
Elastic husky saxophones on tape are stretching
twisting sixties tunes around the smell of coffee.
Morning muesli's over-sweetened by thick honey
of harmonica, condensed milk clarinet.
Mirrors by the bar reverse the consonants
on beer pumps and deflect what ought to be my eyeline.

But even if the alphabets weren't back to front
I'd still not get a glimpse of Lisi. She's not come
or left a note or waft of perfume so she can't
have read my hotel booking, let alone my mind.

It's my own fault of course. I got myself entangled
in a fantasy. There's no way out of this—
unless I find there's someone here who knows the ropes
who'll spare the time to steer me nearer to Tamara.

Well, do you think our little impromptu experiment served its purpose George? Prince enquired, looking hard at Hamblin as soon as the latter had stopped reading.

You ought to ask our audience that, Hamblin responded, reasonably enough. But the audience was not particularly interested. Although one or two people made polite affirmative noises there was a general feeling—even if it was not articulated—that they had all been witnessing some sort of verbal arm-wrestling between the tutors. They had both given the strong impression of regarding certain words and phrases as being loaded with extra meaning. Notwithstanding Prince's impromptu manifesto, Stanley was sure that the events of the last ten minutes had not been for the benefit of the guests—most of whom appeared to be quite ready to break up the gathering and get a good night's sleep in preparation for the week ahead.

Episode 5: Conflicts & surprises on Monday

Since they had all gone to bed fairly early (and fairly sober) Stanley expected his fellow guests to begin the next day with fresh and open-minded attitudes. But Daisie kept on gazing admiringly at Prince and Willoughby soon chose to dig himself deeper into the conversational rut he had opened up the night before. He engaged Prince in a "private" conversation about publishers who *do not even extend the elementary courtesy of replying to letters*. There were sympathetic murmurs from those who could hardly help overhearing; and these encouraged Willoughby to complain specifically of having written to Prince repeatedly about a manuscript he'd submitted to Epidermis Press several months before. *For all I know, you might never have got it. Or else you've lost it: I've heard bad rumours about your office admin.* (An expression on Prince's face suggested there was a foundation for such rumours.)

Hoping to lighten the mood, Mary Maxwell mentioned having once heard of an editor who was so efficient that any poet who dawdled on the way home from posting a submission might well find a rejection waiting on the doormat. Hamblin seized on the diversion. *I think I know which editor you mean and he* was *a bit exceptional! But even he couldn't have been that fast when Eric & I were at Bogburgh. The village post box was in the wall beside our house.* This remark enabled Barry Wigfall to change the subject again and ask if Prince intended to give the group a preview of the new Jessop book. He received only a non-committal reply but at least the awkward moment had passed and the next writing exercise could begin.

***

And did Eric ever have any family? asked Mary Maxwell as she sat next to Hamblin at lunch. Stanley overheard the question and thought it seemed a slightly odd way to phrase it—as if anyone could be in the world without having had some genetic links to other human beings. Presumably the word *ever* was included to make the sentence more satisfying to deliver.

Well he had no brothers or sisters, Hamblin replied. *His parents were both dead by the time I knew him and he never mentioned any aunts or uncles.*

How sad, Mary murmured, *to be the only child of only children.* She made it sound as if this might be as much a source of magical powers as being the seventh son of a seventh son.

After lunch, Abigail and Barry approached Julia to ask whether—in spite of having booked separately—they could now reduce their bill by sharing a room. Julia firmly said this would *not* be possible—at least as far as any cost reduction was concerned. Abigail accepted this with a shrug and switched her attention to a photograph on Julia's desk, observing that its subject looked like Eric Jessop. *Yes,* said Julia, *it was taken when Eric led a course here a year or two before he ... died. The photo was on the desk when I arrived and I left it there because Eric & I knew each other at university and we'd kept in touch, on and off.*

Abigail evidently felt this titbit of information about Julia was something to be shared with the rest of the guests. She told the story several times and Stanley was mildly surprised that she did so without concealing what he would have regarded as the entirely private reason she and Barry had gone see Julia in the first place.

At this stage of the week, conversations between the guests largely consisted of discussions of previous poetic successes and frustrations, interspersed with exchanges of opinions about the tutors. Clearly Daisie and Willoughby had both come to meet

Prince (although for quite different reasons) and had little interest in Hamblin. Mary thought Hamblin's poetry was *sweet* and was professionally approving of his reading style. Abigail and Barry jointly expressed little enthusiasm about either Hamblin or Prince but conceded the importance of gaining access to the literary networks the tutors belonged to. However Barry, on the rare occasions when he was not with Abigail, did admit to enjoying Prince's sinister narratives *even if they are a bit dated*. If he had been asked directly, Stanley would have happily announced that he enjoyed—and sometimes admired—quite a lot of the work of both tutors. But he seldom chose to volunteer his opinions.

Perhaps surprisingly, there was not very much conversational speculation about the newly discovered Eric Jessop manuscript. Willoughby obviously cared about nobody's book except his own, still unpublished, collection. Daisie's interest was in Prince himself rather than his publishing ventures. Barry and Abigail perhaps thought it would seem unsophisticated to admit to any excitement at the prospect of Prince giving the group a preview. Mary and Stanley did talk once or twice about the sadness of Eric's lonely death. Mary clearly knew the story quite well and her account of Eric's wiped-clean computer and two abandoned poems left an impression on Stanley that was as vivid and poignant as the image of sealed doors and open gas oven that he associated with the suicide of Sylvia Plath.

***

The tutors had announced that they would take a back seat in the Monday evening session so the guests could have a chance to read what they considered to be one of their most successfully dark poems. The reading order was decided by drawing names from a hat—although Abigail begged the privilege of going last.

Daisie read first. *The darkest things I can think of,* she said, *are those that cause harm or distress to children.*

QUALITY TIME

My Dad takes me on the bus:
today we're going to the zoo.
He laughs when I pull funny faces—
not like Mum who says they're silly.

Then he starts to ask me lots
of questions about school and things
that happened weeks ago. How many
different teachers have we had
for maths this term? And was it just
the Mayor of Hackney or the proper
Mayor of London at assembly?

Going home, we have a game
of *Guess the teacher's nickname*. He tries
Pat O'Cake and Micky Finn:
and then I think about this evening
when the airport taxi stops
outside our house to take him back
to Belfast.
    He'll be waving to me
and making little funny faces.

It was Stanley's turn next, and this gave some of the guests a chance to hear him say a greater number of consecutive words than he had so far managed in the preceding twenty-four hours at Weald Barn. His guiding principle in life was to avoid speaking except when he knew he had something worth saying. He believed the poem he was offering met that criterion. To introduce it, he simply said that his darkest fears were to do with being betrayed by his own body.

GRAND MAL

Misprints make him restless still
by being not quite wrong. Is this
another tiny crease preceding
total folding of the world
as images from either side
fail to match but dip and slide
attaching half a floating face
to a poster on the wall?

The first time that a book dissolved
before his eyes was in a French class—
a *trompe l'oeil* he might have said
had language not already left him
soundless, dropping like a dead thing,
waking later with no answer
for the problem he'd become.

One consultant re-assured
his parents it could be controlled;
then turned to tell him how he shared
pathology with Caesar and
perhaps as well with Dostoevsky
which scarcely seemed a consolation
for permanent uncertainty.

Sunlight glancing off the sea
disturbs a shining worm that sleeps
behind his eye. And as it swims
it imitates the filament
within the naked bulb he dreads
which hangs beside a door that opens
only inwards and whose sudden
flashing is the final warning
the handle is about to turn.

While some people were wondering if Stanley's poem might be autobiographical, Mary Maxwell stood up, poised and ready to claim the audience's full attention. Her poem was also about bodily frailty but it involved a larger cast of characters and *explored a darker sort of reaction to ill-health.*

MEDICAL HISTORY

At seventeen she lost her balance;
Fell in what she said was love
With a boy who limped. The doctors
Said it would get worse. Her parents,
Doing what was best for her,
Did their best to hobble the relationship,

Whispering they would not want
Her handicapped by being married
To a weakling. What they didn't
Reckon on, or seem to mind,
Was that she might be equally
Disabled by the able-bodied
Older man who strode up to her
Once the cripple had received his marching orders.

And he decided he'd take care
Of all her cares until they vanished.
So, inside ten years, did she;
And after twenty more she couldn't
Turn the tables, wait on him
Once his stewardship was cancelled
When he'd been struck down. She visits
If someone offers her a lift:
She never learned to drive, hates buses
And the Home is farther than she likes to walk.

Barry Wigfall seemed pleased that the running order had given him a chance to jump on an already rolling bandwagon of medical themes. His approach to the subject however was (he said) meant to show that some moments can feel desperately dark while they are happening but, in hindsight, may seem pretty trivial or even comic.

MOVING VIOLATION

Blame it on the shellfish is a simple rule:
maybe bouillabaisse
can imitate an enema?
D & V's a delicate abbreviation
but, taken short in Arles, it was precious little use
to observe I wasn't vomiting.

Often one's unsure what bitter fungus spoiled
a well-intentioned stew.
This time I knew which pinch of mischief
I'd had slipped to me in St Remy that morning:
while I'd picnicked, unsuspectingly, brisk thieves
had vandalised my car.

The gendarme chose to called the damage *dégradation*,
which is what it felt like
as I took in the incident.
Those types who broke the lock undid my intestines,
which testified against them, with a steady stream
of—so to speak—invective.

Willoughby's turn came next. *Well Barry certainly got in among some human fundamentals with that one,* he observed approvingly. *And I suppose mine gets back to basics of another kind—in the darker corners of the male psyche when it starts to doubt itself...*

PHARMACEUTICALS

A T-shaped glimpse of golden thong
above a low-slung denim waistband
catches my attention in the café,
distracts me from my muffin.

From his Hull high window, Larkin
watched, lamenting his exclusion
from the youthful sexfest of the sixties.
Would he be sad to miss
paraded navels, hipbones, hints
of buttock, casual navvy language
blunt-appealing to the loins like forwards
bawling at a linesman?

Some say he liked that sort of thing.
But, now I am at least as old
as he was then, I do begin to wonder
how he might have coped
with such abundant come-ons, even
in his prime when—never mind
librarians' delusions—half-a-chance
could still play hard to get.

Of course The Pill has transformed lives,
but being at it now like knives
must take its toll. Thank Chemists that there are
new pills to keep men up to par.

Finally it was Abigail's turn to justify the "top-of-the-bill" placing she had claimed. She explained that she wanted to present a long poem in three voices. Prince gave a too-obvious sigh at this point. Abigail had already recruited Mary to speak the poem's stage directions while Barry was to supply the voice which came from stage right. Abigail herself delivered the lines from stage left and hence was the last to speak. The trio had evidently done some rehearsing and Mary's professional expertise ensured that the initial scene-setting description generated a pleasantly mysterious and unsettling atmosphere.

SINCEREST FORM

[Time: the present or the recent past.
The place: rural Ontario. Stage lights
go up, reveal a pair of living rooms.
A flimsy curtain (gauze?) is hung between them.
Both have upstage picture windows: one
(the left, untidy) looks out on a lake;
the other (smartly furnished) oversees
a pinewood coloured oatfield, cut from woodland,
with an edge capriciously unstraight
as an amateur's attempt at planking.
Suddenly the left hand lights go down.]

*It started with my hearthrug
whose muted colours you admired*

[Sound of footsteps and the sudden scrape
of wood on wood within the darkened room.]

*A copy of my easy chair
appeared beside your fire,
one foot resting on that piece
of duplicated kilim.*

*I often told you how I found it
comfortable. Which I did
and which it was. And still remains.*

*I did not see your curtains,
replicating mine, till winter
evenings drew them closed.*

*I never failed to draw attention
to my fifties reproduction
of your Georgian chaise-longue.*

*You could not catalogue my books
and yet you built their shelves
along your walls, emulsion-painted
to match the five-year aging
of my Regency matt olive.*

[A laboured rendering of *"Für Elise"*
can be heard played softly from offstage]

                    As a non-musician,
                    why acquire a grand piano?

It was left me by an aunt.
But I don't suppose you knew
I saw the Bechstein's keys turn plastic
at your touch; your hands become
immersed in music to the wrists.

    [Piano music stops. Re-lit, both rooms
        now appear to be identical—
  but the window views are as they were.]

                    And why desire an ersatz version
                                of my living space?

I could not imitate your portraits—
least of all your English uncle
posing in his Old School tie.

                You're wrong. It is my British cousin
                    twice removed, whose picture
                      you are mis-remembering.
                            He wrote mysteries,
            setting them in country houses
                    in the thirties, blending
                    kedgeree with evidence.

Perhaps I meant to dramatise
an inverse alibi: a false
location where a witness
at a vital time will swear
you weren't at home. "But I was there,"
they will insist "and he was not!"

Or possibly I'll drug and lull
a victim who's afraid to trust me
yet will think they're safe with you.

Or maybe you are my intended
victim. After all. This time.

        [A single gunshot. Then slow fade to black.]

Or was it that I wanted you
to feel you were at home with me?

What the hell was that about? Prince muttered to Julia—too loudly—as they left the room together after polite applause had greeted the end of Abigail's poem. Stanley thought this was rather a churlish and thoughtless comment since he himself had enjoyed the enigmatic narrative and its unusual presentation. It turned out, however, that Prince's disapproval was not confined to poetic issues. He continued his grumbling to Julia by saying *that young woman has a way of putting herself in the limelight and getting people to jump through hoops for her.* Abigail, within earshot of both remarks, flushed with anger.

Episode 6: Setbacks & tensions on Tuesday

Stanley had been looking forward to his Tuesday late-morning tutorial with Hamblin. Behind his shyness he was quietly confident that his poetry was as well-crafted as his mathematics. Hence he was expecting mainly encouraging comments while hoping for some hints on how to make his work even better. But he was to be gravely disappointed. When he came down from Hamblin's room he was red-faced and had traces of tears in his eyes. *Crossword clues, relentlessly iambic, obsessed with patterns! What kind of constructive criticism is that?* he asked Mary and Daisie plaintively. They agreed that such remarks did seem needlessly ungracious. Daisie added that she'd noticed Hamblin being very irritable earlier in the day when he'd gone to the office to see Julia Nelson and found Prince already there—*such a small thing to get upset about!*

Willoughby's turn to have a one-to-one meeting with Prince came immediately after lunch. He had brought a copy of his manuscript and evidently expected a full appraisal—preferably followed by an offer of publication. Prince may or may not have tried to be helpful; but Willoughby appeared unable to accept any criticism. His loudest protests could be overheard in the lounge—as could Prince's eventual damning verdict *All right, if you really want to press me then the decision is no!*

For the rest of the afternoon, Mary watched with amusement as Willoughby and Stanley tried repeatedly to get a quiet word with (respectively) Hamblin and Prince—presumably in the hope that one tutor would supply some ointment to soothe the wounds inflicted by the other. Stanley complained to Daisie that he found Prince particularly elusive. *He spends far too much time hanging around that Julia,* Daisie remarked bitterly. *She should tell him—it's us he's meant to be paying attention to.*

Oddly enough, Willoughby—when he wasn't trying to corner Hamblin—could also have been accused of "hanging around" Julia. Stanley had often seen him hovering near her office; and once when she asked him directly if he was looking for her, he replied, with heavy-handed gallantry, *no—but I can't imagine why I wasn't!* Whenever Julia joined the guests for evening drinks, Willoughby frequently focussed his gaze on her attractively severe features and dark wavy hair.

***

The anxieties of Stanley and Willoughby were obviously of small concern to other people. But there was still enough tension in the air at the evening reading for the tutors to try and lighten the atmosphere by asking the guests for some humorous offerings. *Black humour would be best, of course,* observed Prince. *And we won't have a pre-set running order this time so please feel free to chip in whenever you think your poem will fit…*

Willoughby started the ball rolling with a quasi-haiku called "Genesis":

> *Mouth still full of fruit*
> *Eve said to Adam "You need*
> *a bigger fig leaf."*

This proved to be an all-too-appropriate curtain raiser for his longer poem.

MEMOIRS OF A FXXX-HUNTING MAN

I probably owe Bobby Oates a fiver.
I bet him he'd not get his end away
before he married. And that nor would I.
In 1962, I thought, with Larkin,
sexual intercourse had not begun
and I was sure no-one in Middlesex
was bedding anyone they were not wed to—
in spite of whispers about Beryl Bone
in the back seat of her Daddy's Sunbeam.

(So, on Sundays in her room, Lorraine
and I would play "Taboo" and "Ev'rything
I've Got Belongs to You" by Charlie Byrd
while both remaining technically virgins.)

I'd wager now I lost my wager when
Eileen and Bob went travelling in Wales:
how could he have six nights away with her
and not come home a winner? I'm afraid
I never asked him if he did—not even
after my frayed innocence had lost
all elasticity and slid around
my ankles as I jumped the gun with Gwen.
(Oates should have a fiver for that too.)

It was Mary Maxwell who rose to the challenge of following Willoughby's sexist material. She did so very professionally, reading her poem in a well-assumed Yorkshire accent, evidently untroubled by the risk of offending Barry's native ear.

&

Every Friday Walt & Iris came to Bert & Flo's,
Played cards and had a beer or two—
Except when Flo said sherry for the ladies.
They'd chat about the way their week had gone
Settled in on Bert & Flo's plush three-piece suite.

Then Iris died and went up to the Crem
With Walt & Bert & Flo & other friends
In big black cars. So Walt came by himself
On Fridays and they took to playing crib instead of solo.

When Walt bumped into Betty at the Co-op
Once or twice, they started going out
To quiet pubs where no one knew them—
Till they showed their faces in Walt's local.

The thing was, Walt had been with Elsie once—
Oh, years ago when they were young—
And she'd died too. And that's when Iris came along
To sort Walt out. He'd been a mess
And Iris was the saving of him—that was why
Most folk were always fine with Walt & Iris...
But Walt & Betty—after all that Iris did for him—
That wasn't right, it was too soon and anyway
It wouldn't work.

        When Walt & Betty called
On Bert & Flo one Friday, Flo made sandwiches
And cups of tea. They talked about the weather
And the underpass; and when they left
Bert whispered as he shook Walt's hand
I shouldn't bother bringing her again.

Daisie stood up next. *This one's about children again*, she said. *I love the way their innocence can disarm even dark things.*

PRIMARY COLOURING

A rich *melange* of red and yellow,
damp in parts, is corrugating
as it dries. "So what's it called?" I ask.
Wrong question. For a six year-old
a painting's all about sensation
not portrayal. All the same
she humours me and lucky-dips
a pair of referents. "It's blood,"
she says "and melted butter"
daring me to disagree.

Stanley, with a meaningful sidelong glance at Hamblin, explained that his poem would involve *iambic permutations and combinations of a finite set* consisting of words from a well-known song lyric by Gerald Marks & Seymour Simons.

ALL OF ME

Once I was all heart. That left no part
I'll never lose to you. Was I to go
My left arm's all that I can part with? No!
So use me; use me how you want to!
Take the part I'll never use without you!
Part your wanton lips and cry
Go on! Go on! That was so good!

Eyes see; eyes want; arms take; arms use;
lips go *goodbye, dear*—that was you
with me. That was how to lose me.
Without heart, your *I'm so good to you*
was cant. You never took my wants to heart.
You never took me to see *Can-Can*—
not the good part. All you left to me
was left to go with out-takes to the can.

If Stanley's poem had surprised everyone else by venturing into Willoubghby-like (or at least Willoughby-lite) territory then Abigail's offering turned out to be even more unexpected. It revealed a capacity for humour at odds with the fierce intensity of the work she had previously shared. *The darkest aspect of this poem for me,* she said, smiling, *is the fact that Country & Western music exists at all!*

RHYME, REGRET & IRRATIONAL OPTIMISM IN CANADIAN COUNTRY & WESTERN LYRICS

Dust is rising up beside the highway
where a John Deere tractor grumbles by;
but since your Dear John letter headed my way
dust is not the thing that stings my eye

and blurs Alberta highway to a cry-way
through a windshield streaked and smeared with tears.
The road I'm riding now is a goodbye-way
that runs away from all our happy years.

This would have been a straight and clear dry-eye way
if only I'd been driving back to you;
but I've detoured onto a groan-and-sigh way—
one bad mistake means you and I are through.

Red roofs of Red Deer are coming nearer
and after that it's Edmonton ahead.
I'm pushing onward up to Athabasca
where I was born and might as well be dead.

This used to be my gravy-and-meat-pie way:
white propane tanks bunched up in fields like sheep
would soothe me in a kind-of-lullaby way
when I came home to eat with you and sleep.

You're angry in a like-to-see-me-fry way.
You're telling me that my behaviour stinks
in a told-another-girl-I'd-be-her-guy way
because I'd had a few too many drinks.

As I'm getting near Leduc I nearly puke—
I'm gagging, dragging ragged hopes up north.
I'm like a runner, dreaming of a medal,
missing out on bronze and coming fourth.

Last week this was my I'll-be-warm-and-dry way
with you at home to keep me safe and calm:
now it's the I'll-be-living-in-a-sty way
that takes me back to Daddy's sad old farm.

    The final spot in this session now belonged to Barry Wigfall. His performance, unsurprisingly, involved Abigail who, still in flippant mood, provided primly-spoken footnotes to his "translation". *Until Abigail came along I've never had a chance to recite this poem*, Barry announced enthusiastically.

IN SAN GIMIGNANO[1]

from the C 17th original Italian by Bartolomeo Grande[2]

I feel my heart and codpiece bulge
with admiration for the noble members
of the Tuscan aristocracy!
They have put their mighty erections
in every imaginable passage of our city
to prick the sky, uncircumscribed
by petty protests of the prudish priest
whose sighs did not matter.

Heroes expose the feeble phallacies[3]
of modesty and mock them as a ring master
baits a caged and humbled beast.
When such men bring out their entourage
upon the public streets, tossing
offers[4] to the crowds, they hold themselves
as stiffly as befits their rank and standing,
riding to the rhythm of the heavy throb
of drums made with four skins[5]
while minstrels sing the praises of their wan king[6],[7].

[1] Called the town of 1000 towers for very obvious reasons
[2] Merely to dub this poet as "obscure" might be to flatter him unduly
[3] An attempt to capture an archaic spelling in the original
[4] Possibly it was a custom for noblemen seeking retainers to throw letters of invitation to promising young men
[5] Evidently a technical term in instrument manufacture

⁶ *Il pallido sovrano* seems to have been a legendary hero to whom some Tuscan nobles chose to profess allegiance. This may have been a convenient ruse for avoiding the political risks of total loyalty to a living leader who was always liable to be displaced.

Space precludes a full account of the deeds and virtues of this mythical pale ruler but it may be of some interest to note that he is said to have relied heavily for his authority upon a shadowy companion *Bottone*⁷ who possessed *una bacchetta meravigliosa*—a rod of extraordinary significance and power. It is hardly necessary to draw attention to parallels with the figure of Merlin in Arthurian legend (or, as some scholars observe, with Aaron in the Judaeo-Christian tradition).

⁷ It is not easy to render this name into English in a way that sounds suitably impressive. However the blunt translation "Knob" may be preferred to the more colloquial "Nobby" since it can be taken to mean the centre or boss of a shield and hence signify the role of protector. (A more fanciful theory proposes a link with the folk tale of Cinderella.)

Barry had arranged matters so that Abigail only had to interrupt the poem for footnotes 3 & 4. Footnotes 1 & 2 were delivered in a pause after the title while 5, 6 & 7 were saved for the end. Their *bravura* performance was a great success and even Hamblin seemed able to set his grumpiness aside enough to laugh out loud at the cumulative pseudo-academic nonsense in the final footnotes. Some of the guests declared this piece of straightforward ribaldry to be the high spot of the workshop so far.

Episode 7: Provocations & reactions on Wednesday

The Bible tells us that *A merry heart doeth good like a medicine* (Proverbs 17) and Stanley certainly found that his enjoyment of Tuesday night's genuinely funny poems helped him to sleep well and to shake off much of his disappointment at Hamblin's negative opinion of his work. For Hamblin himself, however, any brief lifting of his bad mood did not seem to have helped him find a better side of the bed to get out of on Wednesday. During the morning he turned his forceful criticisms on Abigail, telling her quite bluntly that her work was *too self-absorbed, too Canadian, and excluded the British reader*. Abigail was particularly upset by his dismissive treatment of the longer sequence from which Monday's *ensemble* piece "Sincerest Form" had been taken. That sequence was very important to her, dealing as it did with episodes in the mental breakdown of her much-loved father. Hamblin's criticisms were especially hard to bear, coming on top of Prince's off-the-cuff disparaging remarks on Monday night. Abigail's distress at this verdict was expressed with more defiance than Stanley had shown the day before—but she was probably helped in this by Barry's loyal readiness to scowl at both tutors on her behalf.

***

Wednesday night marked the mid-point of the workshop and Julia had, as usual, invited a guest reader. On this occasion it was Seth Buckler—a self-proclaimed Kentish man who liked to compare himself to Wat Tyler as an aggressive representative of the common people. (Stanley refrained from mentioning that, strictly speaking, Tyler could actually have been a Man of Kent by virtue of being born east of the Medway.)

Buckler was well-known as a confrontational performer; but it was nevertheless a surprise when he preceded his reading with a string of semi-jocular disparaging remarks about both the resident tutors. He made mild fun of Prince's *prep school dormitory ghost stories* but for some reason he was more scornful of Hamblin's *middle-class nostalgia poems* and informed the audience that the Tunbridge Wells Conservative Club had recently offered a copy of Hamblin's latest collection as first prize in a raffle. *The second prize*, he added, *was two copies.*

Buckler's first poem was a throwaway haiku, called "The Boot Boy & his Mistress" *which shows how the ruling classes have never placed any value on workers*

> *If I don't clean them,*
> *she's cross. If I do, she thinks*
> *they've not got dirty.*

He then turned to the subject of his impatience with the current government for merely *talking about banning hunting instead of simply* doing *it.*

THE FOX-HUNTING BAN

Me, I'd set the dogs on 'em—
their own of course. I'd never let
my own hounds get their honest jaws
caught up in sweaty flesh pretending
to be country bred but rotting
with corruption under fancy coats
and riding sleek entitlements.

There's nature's ways of getting rid of vermin
on your own, on foot that leave you cold
and dirty. Then there's city tricks
of bully-boys who buy results
with bribes so they'll feel dry and clean.

Like I said, I'd set the dogs on them…
But first I'd tie a squirrel tail
to every riding-breeches arse
and watch it waggle as they ran away.

    Buckler chuckled at his own closing image then moved on quickly to *a kind of prose-poem—because there's nothing poetic about the ingredients!*

SEWAGE & MONEY—SPOT THE DIFFERENCE

Both have long been unavoidably involved
                    in any human enterprise;
but until recently it was not done to mention
                    either in mixed company.
We all need early years' tuition in what to do
                    and not to do with both.
It's when we part with some we're most aware
                    how much we have of either.
Vast amounts of both proceed through channels
                    out of sight
and unremarked upon until the flow
                    of either is disrupted.
So experts in the large-scale oversight of both
                    should be rewarded
for their heroic efforts at unblocking
                    either overdrafts or overflows.
Surely both prestige and lavish pay
                    are equally appropriate
for anyone who either builds portfolios
                    or puts up Portaloos.
That's why so many graduates,
                    in both the arts and sciences,
seek lucrative careers in handling
                    either wealth or filth.

    Buckler, sounding more and more like a stand-up comic, turned his attention to the government's new minimum wage. *It's too low of course, but it'll be a start—so long as the "party of business" don't get back in. But if that happens it'll be goodbye to any safeguards on wages or benefits for "scroungers"... Anyway here's a couple about the rich taking care of number one before they screw the rest of us...*

A FINANCIER RESISTS THE STATUTORY MINIMUM WAGE

It's all about
maintaining differentials
don't you see?
To earn my salary
and bonus shares
I have to get up early,
come to London
from deep in rural Surrey—
or my weekend *pied a terre* in Normandy—

and stare at screens
of unforgiving figures,
keep my ear
close to gossip's groundswell
always fearful
in case a tiny slip
of mouth or mouse-click gives anything away.

Why live like that
except for due reward?
If I could make
the same amount by staying
close to home
to empty litter bins
or clean out drains
or wash the elderly I'd do it like a shot.

But then who'd bother
taking time to care about the markets?

BRANDING

Deploying rules and retributions
to eliminate, along with criminals,
the unproductive and inept
is like a stockman using whips
and goads and fences to corral
whatever cattle he may find
unsatisfactory.

Though not himself a quadruped
he's able to identify
the lame, the lean and the diseased
for herding into one small (shrinking) pen
to leave the wider prairie free
for pasturing the prime grade beef
on its polished hooves.

And secretly we all know,
do we not, which side
of those rough posts and rails
we could be standing on.

    As soon as Buckler finished his reading—which most guests seemed to enjoy—Hamblin, evidently still smarting from earlier jibes, snappishly challenged Buckler to admit he was *little more than a champagne socialist playing with radical words while making a nice living as a journalist. And more of a journalist than a poet,* he elaborated. *What was the subtitle on your latest book? "Few & Neglected" wasn't it? Can we persuade you to stop writing by offering a prize for "Best Last Collection"?*
    Stanley did not enjoy confrontation and began to be worried that he was about to witness an ugly scene.

Episode 8: A timely distraction

Before Hamblin's rudeness (or Buckler's reaction) could get out of hand, Prince stepped in with a diversion in the form of an impromptu preview of the rediscovered Eric Jessop collection. *I think I've been clutching it a bit too tightly; so now it's quite hard to share with anyone else. But this feels like a good moment to do it.*

After revealing that the title was "An Image on the Retina", Prince admitted that the reason for the book's delayed appearance was that he had misplaced the manuscript without even knowing he had received it! *Rumours about my poor office management aren't entirely untrue.* Evidently Jessop's package had slipped behind a filing cabinet without being opened and had only come to light during a major spring clean. *Once I realised what it was, it took me a while to deal with it. It was like an unsolicited submission from beyond the grave! It can still shock me even now*

Having created a suitably expectant atmosphere, he began to read.

RE-READING *NINETEEN EIGHTY-FOUR*

I wept when he maintained he'd not betrayed her:
I was just fourteen and could have claimed the same
while sharing Winston's strange affection for O'Brien
who understood how little is admitted
in owning to rebellion below the waist.

She'd kept her feelings for him close and tight
enough to emphasise her shapely hips.
If only she and he had only trusted no one else
they'd not have met again with straggling hair
and no apologies to stare into each other's failure.

I wept when he said baldly he'd betrayed her.
and when she said she'd sold him out as well—
well I of course forgave her. I was just fourteen:
in my revised edition, she was innocent,
her confession all pretence to save his face.

Sitting at this dismal café table now
it comes to me how strongly you resemble her
but I can only guess how fiercely you resent
the state we've reached—both cheated by the same O'Brien
who after all and all the time has been in charge

and called the shots that echo and will echo
down a hall with numbered doors we have to pass.

I am not fourteen and now's the time to tell you
there is no O'Brien and no cage of rodents.

You weep because we know there's only me.

At first nobody spoke. Perhaps no one knew how to react. Was applause appropriate? Or one of those wordless and ambiguous murmurs that sometimes emanate from a poetry audience? The person to break the silence was Mary Maxwell who said—in tones suggesting no contradiction was permitted—*That's a confession by someone who knows they've hurt another person very deeply.*

The second response was more startling. It came from Hamblin who said loudly but calmly *Well, if no one else is going to say it then I will. Eric didn't write that. You've told us how you* claim *you got these poems—but I know they didn't come from Eric! He hardly wrote anything in his last few months—I was there! You've waited till now to peddle some fakes, hoping we'll have forgotten the real thing.*

Prince's reply was both confident and conciliatory. *George, I can see why you're upset. If Eric didn't show you these poems I can understand you being hurt—and even wanting to deny they're genuine. But they are. I've still got the envelope they came in—and the covering letter with Eric's writing.* He waved a piece of paper in Hamblin's direction. Hamblin made a grab for it but Prince easily evaded his clutching hand. Julia moved next to Prince as if to shield him; and Prince, possibly embarrassed by her protectiveness, said gruffly *Look George, let's not go on with this. We've all had a bit too much to drink if truth be told. I probably shouldn't have sprung the poems on you tonight without giving you a chance to see them.*

Hamblin ignored him and stamped out of the room saying he refused to be *party to a con trick.* Strangely it was Seth Buckler who followed him, calling out *Hang on George! Calm down—come and have a drink* (which hardly seemed an appropriate invitation even if well meant).

Julia broke the awkward silence with a trite remark about *artistic temperament.* Her professional manner then cracked as she said *I'm really sorry there's all this bad feeling about poor Eric's book. We were friends at university—only casual friends—I knew he was, well, gay of course—but we'd meet for coffee or at the jazz club now and again. He was good company and he didn't show off when he started winning poetry prizes; so I don't think he'd have wanted people to argue about him.* Whatever that means *"I don't think he'd have wanted ..." He doesn't want anything now!* She turned toward Prince and glanced at the papers in his hand. *And for what it's worth, the big scrawly PS on that letter* does *look like one of his scribbled notes.*

With a mumbled acknowledgement, Prince hastily shoved the papers back into a folder as if wanting to push away recent events along with them.

Most of the tension had abated when Hamblin left the room and there was now an anti-climactic silence which nobody knew how to fill. The guests drifted away from the lounge, going either to the bar or out into the pleasant spring night air.

Episode 9: Shocking discoveries on Thursday

Simply by virtue of showing restraint under provocation, Prince had come out better than Hamblin from the acrimonious Wednesday night exchanges. But neither tutor came out well on Thursday morning. That is to say, both failed to appear at breakfast; and neither had emerged when the first session was due to start. It was Stanley who went to report the absences to Julia. She, already looking tense, assumed managerial responsibility and went up to Prince's room on the first landing. Stanley followed at a distance in a gesture of diffident support. When her knocking went unanswered, Julia tried the door and, on finding it unlocked, turned the handle and stepped inside, calling out Prince's first name as she did so. Stanley had been edging closer and hence was only a few steps away when Julia screamed.

Recent renovations at Weald Barn had created an *en-suite* bedroom from what had once been a bathroom. An old-fashioned wall-mounted roller towel remained from the room's former purpose. Prince was hanging from the loop of this towel, slumped at a shallow angle so that most of his weight rested on his throat, compressing the windpipe and carotid artery. It looked very much as if he was dead.

Stanley reacted with surprising but logical directness, telling Julia to telephone for an ambulance. The other guests had come part way up the stairs on hearing Julia's scream. *An accident—he's had an accident,* Julia stammered as she pushed past them, to get to her office. *Is he hurt?* asked one of the women. *Does he need help?*

That last question should probably have prompted Stanley to call the other men to help lift Prince down, in case his life could be saved. But what Stanley actually did was continue on his own to climb the next flight of stairs to Hamblin's room in the oast-house roof-space. The first thing he saw on reaching the upper landing was a torn piece of paper stuck to Hamblin's door. He paused to read the handwriting on it: *George has jumped the gun again—he should have waited not shot straight back—can't stop this fait accompli now—time for a quick exit...*

Both alarmed and puzzled by this, Stanley called out *Mr Hamblin!* and entered the room without knocking. There was a strong smell of whisky. Hamblin was lying on the bed. Only his legs and body were visible at first, everything above the chest being hidden by a bedside table. But when Stanley moved nearer, he was shocked to see Hamblin's head completely (and horribly) enclosed in a black plastic bin-liner, the drawstring tight around his neck. There was an empty glass by the bed and some white pills were strewn around it. Stanley remembered reading somewhere that self-asphyxiation following drug-induced unconsciousness is the second best method of suicide (hanging being the most effective).

Few people can predict—or would even think in advance about—how they might react when faced with one sudden death, let alone two. As Stanley backed away from the distressing sight his shoe brushed against a loosely crumpled ball of paper, sending it skittering across the floor. Some impulse of tidiness made him pick it up. As he did so he suddenly realised he must tell someone about this second fatality so he stuffed the paper in his pocket and clattered downstairs with the grim news.

Ambulances came (in vain) followed closely by police cars. While investigations began, the shocked guests, along with the badly-shaken Julia, were allowed to stay in the lounge, any comings and goings loosely monitored by a uniformed constable.

Conversation was at first directed toward putting some sort of narrative together. Stanley of course could supply the most complete account of events. While not going into great detail about the ugliness of the two corpses, he could repeat more or less *verbatim* the mysterious message on Hamblin's door.

A collective attempt to work out who-was-where at the end of the previous evening was not very successful because nobody seemed to have stayed in one place for very long. It was agreed that Prince had gone upstairs with his papers; but he could easily have come back down later without being noticed. None of the guests could remember seeing Hamblin again after his dramatic exit. He might or might not have quickly shaken off Seth Buckler; but since Buckler had not stayed overnight he could not be asked. Nobody had observed Buckler leaving the premises.

Although Julia had seemed much friendlier with Prince than with Hamblin, it was the latter's death that appeared to cause her greater distress. She kept saying *But I gave him the bag, I gave him the bag!* It emerged that Hamblin had come to her office at around midnight, while she was *catching up on endless paperwork*. He said he was looking for a rubbish sack because he had spilled a bottle of whisky on his desk and had used a whole box of tissues to mop up the mess. *He seemed really agitated and asked if I could sell him another bottle. Well I couldn't do that, but I did go to the bar and serve him a triple whisky in a glass. If only I hadn't done that…*

Once it was clear there were no more hard facts to work with, conjectures began to bounce to and fro across the lounge in several voices…

So Poetry can Make Something Happen!
    Two Somethings even!
           That's not very funny.
   And who says it's about poetry?
It must be because of last night's row.
      That was nothing to get suicidal over!
   Well, what if the Jessop book's a fake & Prince
   panicked when Hamblin saw straight through it?
OK, I suppose that's possible …
    And Prince would be finished If he
    got caught out in a fraud like that…
      Yes, but he didn't look *very panicky!*
Agreed! So the book's not *a fake.*
      But whether it's a fake or not,

> *why did* Hamblin *kill himself?*
>
> *Well if it's genuine, Hamblin has to
> face that Eric was lying to him*
>
> *Yes, that could be very hurtful for him*
>
> *But Hamblin's note didn't mention Eric*
>
> *Maybe he was too upset
> to make sense?*
>
> *OK—if the book's genuine it upsets Hamblin;
> then why does* Prince *kill himself?*
>
> *Exactly! But he* did *kill himself
> so it* proves *the book's a fake!*
>
> *What if the book's a fake & Prince
> loses his nerve; but then Hamblin starts
> thinking it* could *be genuine after all
> That way they could* both *be suicidal.*
>
> *You're still ignoring Hamblin's note!
> What does "jumped the gun" mean?*
>
> *Well he did jump in pretty fast
> with claiming the book's a fraud*
>
> *That's true. He'd only heard one poem.*
>
> *And the way he acted actually made
> me want to side with Prince…*
>
> *Me too. And Hamblin probably
> realised that himself later on.*
>
> *So the "fait accompli" bit means he
> thought he'd botched his protest
> and let Prince get away with it?*
>
> *What, just because he mistimed
> his challenge? That's ridiculous!*
>
> *Of course it is. But if that's how he* felt
> *it could have made him suicidal.*

Daisie Blake had taken no part in these speculations. Indeed she had hardly spoken since the bodies were discovered and was now aimlessly flicking through books she picked at random from the shelves. Suddenly she cried out *Oh no! This is awful!* Turning to the rest of the group she said *Listen to what I've found in one of George Hamblin's old collections. It's so prophetic, but* it's the wrong person… Her eyes filled with tears as she began to read.

DON'T TRY THIS AT HOME

I could have been a footnote in a lot of lives—the boy
they went to school with and who killed himself
when he was twelve and told nobody why.

Prowling through the house alone, my boredom
saw the kitchen towel looped round its roller on the door
and impulse simply slipped my head through,
letting time hang heavy on my jugular and wind-pipe.

A helicopter squatted on my skull with swishing rotors;
then private stars and pleasant pins-and-needles
accompanied my standing up and coming back
to atmospheric and hydraulic normal.

I tried that buzz again, pushed dizziness a little harder.
Then harder still. I next remember cool red tiles beneath my cheek,
my limbs spread artlessly and ready for the chalk-line.

Two frayed ends of shabby fabric drooped like angel wings
above me. Mum's worn argument against the playground's grime—
so often rendered grubby by my botched and cursory ablutions—
had failed at last and failed to let me wash my hands of life.

Grimly relevant though it might have seemed, this childhood recollection from Hamblin's back catalogue added nothing useful to the group's speculations. By late afternoon—when the guests were told they must stay at Weald Barn for one more night while further evidence was collected and full statements were taken—Stanley was tired of recycled and unsystematic theorising. He went to his room to tackle the problem by himself and in his own way.

Episode 10: Stanley reads a letter

Once he was alone, Stanley began analysing the puzzle again from the beginning. At first glance it appeared that the two deaths were suicides. But was it likely that Prince and Hamblin had both reached an unbearable crisis on the same night? Neither death could be an accident—unless, perhaps, Prince had read Hamblin's roller-towel poem and been tempted to replicate the experience! So might at least one of the deaths be murder disguised as suicide? And, if so, what could be the motive? Undoubtedly Prince and Hamblin were at odds over both the Jessop manuscript and the McMahon residency: but was either issue important enough to lead to violence? To clarify matters, Stanley began writing in his notebook.

> *Suppose x killed P and y killed H.*
> *If we reject $x=P, y=H$ (double suicide)*
> *and $x=H, y=P$ (impossible!) then*
> *EITHER (i) $x=y=H$ or $y=x=P$ (murder followed by suicide)*
> *OR (ii) $x \mathbin{/}= H$ and/or $y \mathbin{/}= P$*
> *(i.e. a third—and possibly a fourth—party is involved)*

As regards case (ii), Stanley's observations of the other guests enabled him easily to jot down some values for x and y along with corresponding motives. As he did so, he wondered why it felt natural to refer to some people only by their surnames while others merited a first-name. (But he evidently failed to note that his reason for including $y=Abigail$ was equally a reason to consider $y=Stanley$ (or *Spenser*)).

$x = Willoughby?$ *(P's unprofessional & harsh handling of his poems)*;
$x = Daisie?$ *(P spurning her flirtatious advances)*;
x and/or $y = Abigail?$ *(P & H both scornful about important poems)*
x and/or $y = Barry?$ *(Solidarity/complicity with Abigail?)*
$y = Seth\ Buckler?$ *(Public rudeness to H reflects some deeper issue??)*

Willoughby's long-standing grievance against Prince provided the most plausible (or least implausible) motive. But who could tell how much Daisie had invested in hopes of a romantic liaison with Prince? (The cliché *Hell hath no fury* …insisted on crossing Stanley's mind.) It was harder to imagine murder resulting from a few critical comments: but Abigail was undoubtedly an intense young woman who must have been deeply hurt by the tactless dismissal of poems about her father. Might she (with Barry's help?) have planned a retaliatory practical joke that went horribly wrong? Seth Buckler's 'motive' was pure conjecture; but he *was* one of the last people to be seen with Hamblin and his later movements remained unclear. The one person who seemed to have no motive of any sort was Mary Maxwell. *So if this were a detective story*, Stanley reflected, *she'd have to be the culprit!*

Stanley paced up and down his small room trying to recollect any incident from the past few days that might be significant. His memories however were dominated by unpleasant images of the dead tutors. Fortunately his involuntary recall of what he had seen in Hamblin's room suddenly reminded him of the piece of paper he had picked up from the floor. Taking it from his pocket he looked at it for the first time. It was the torn top part of a typewritten letter. And, as he read it, he found it acting like a set of points to switch his train of thought onto an entirely different track.

Bogburgh Cottage 16/4/95

Well, Stephen, this new manuscript may surprise you. I've been working on it pretty much in secret because George gets grumpy if he sees me writing while he's only churning out reviews and angling for residencies. (And he's drinking too much.) So while he's off in Piddlecombe-in-the-Wold, or wherever, I'm going to finish this draft and stick it in the post before he gets back tomorrow. Of course, if you publish it I'll have to find a way of breaking the news to George—but for now I'll keep my copy of the mss well out of sight ...

Obviously this was part of the covering letter for the lost-and-found Eric Jessop manuscript. Interestingly, it confirmed the manuscript's authenticity while also explaining Hamblin's scepticism about it. But how had it come to be on the floor of Hamblin's room? Why was it torn? And where was the rest of it?

Stanley remembered that, during the previous evening's arguments, either Prince or Julia had mentioned a postscript to Eric's letter. This must have been written on the missing part of the torn page Stanley was now holding. So could that torn-off half page—complete with Eric's scribbled postscript—have been used to make the note that was stuck to Hamblin's door?

It wasn't possible, of course, to compare the two pieces of paper; the police would have taken the note from Hamblin's door as evidence. Indeed, they would also have had the letter if Stanley had done the proper thing and left it for them to find. But rather than wasting time on recriminations, he turned to a new question: if the note on Hamblin's door really was the missing PS then what could Eric have meant by saying Hamblin had *jumped the gun* and that a *quick exit* was called for?

It was easy to guess an answer. Eric had planned to send off his manuscript while Hamblin was away; so if his partner returned sooner than expected, the package would need to be posted quickly. And that *could* be done because—as Hamblin had explained during Monday's discussion about editorial tardiness—there was a pillar box very near the Bogburgh cottage. Eric could easily have slipped out by the front door, while Hamblin was putting the car away, say, or taking luggage upstairs.

Stanley's rational mind winced at the illogicality of someone being in a hurry to post a letter and yet choosing to waste time by adding a PS to an already typed letter saying he was acting in a hurry! Perhaps such muddled thinking was a symptom of the depression that eventually led to Eric's death ...

... but wait a minute! You can't be depressed about writer's block when you're writing a covering letter to go with a new collection!

So Eric's fatal depression must have started some time *after* he had written this letter. Perhaps it was triggered by Prince telling him the manuscript wasn't good enough? But, no, that couldn't be right either: Eric never had a reply from Prince because the letter and manuscript got lost in the Epidermis office!

Was it then the *lack* of response to his poems that caused Eric to slide into depression? How long did he wait for Prince's answer—the one that never came? How much time elapsed between the writing of this letter and Eric's tragic death? Or, putting it more bluntly, *How long did it take for Eric to become desperate enough to kill himself?*

The answer to that grim question might lie in Eric's posthumously published *Collected Poems*. Stanley went down to the library to look for a copy.

Episode 11: A question of dates

When Stanley arrived at the library he was surprised to find Julia already there. He was even more surprised to see she was reading the same Eric Jessop collection that he had come for. *Great minds think alike,* he said rather lamely; *I wanted to look at something in that book too.* He didn't want to explain what it was and fortunately Julia didn't ask. She simply said *listen to this* and began to read

> Planets curve in orbits under forces
> of attraction. Lovers trace two courses—
> both eccentric—round one proposition
> *we're in love,* and may reach opposition:
> if a full diameter divides them
> empty darkness, stretched between them, hides them.
> At my perigee—when I'm most close to
> focussing on you—you're not supposed to
> be so distant.   Apogee's a chance
> for looking back on what should be a dance
> and not a race. Don't Newton's laws ordain
> that if one waits the other one must gain?
> So time itself, in time, can synchronize
> our passions with each sunset and sunrise.

It's called "Emotional Trajectories" she said. *Even when Eric was being playfully "poetic" he could still say real and serious things.* She closed the book. *You can have it now if you like. I've only been browsing it as the next best thing to Eric's lost manuscript. I wish I'd grabbed that last night when I had the chance. Now the police must have taken it and I don't suppose I'll ever see Eric's final poems.*

Stanley thought Julia was being too pessimistic, but she dismissed his attempts at reassurance. *No, think about it—with Eric and Stephen and George all dead, who owns the manuscript? I don't think Eric had any relatives; and why would anyone else try for the publication rights? It's not as if there'd be a fortune to be made.*

Not my problem—or yours, thought Stanley; but Julia was becoming more upset. *It's all such a miserable mess,* she went on. *Poor Eric not knowing his collection had got lost and worrying why Stephen didn't reply. And then the awful breakdown in his relationship with George—by the end they obviously weren't communicating at all. Stephen told me George never really understood Eric; and George must have kept on blaming himself after Eric was dead. I saw that awful suicide note he left; and the way he referred to himself in the third person shows he was still full of self-loathing.*

Stanley was only half-listening to Julia's words. He was much more interested in trying to find an answer to his own question about the date of Eric's death. So he was pleased when she broke off and said *Sorry I'm going on a bit.* She handed him the book and left.

As soon as Stanley opened Eric's *Collected Poems*, the first few words of the preface told him what he wanted to know: *On April 17th 1995, the body of Eric Jessop was discovered...*

But this was not the answer he had expected. Stanley had taken it for granted that Eric's death had occurred a good many months after the posting of the manuscript of his final collection. But now it was clear that he had been wrong. The date on the torn letter plainly showed that it had been written on the day before Eric's body was found—which must have been the very day of his death! This was a startlingly grim discovery and—as Stanley now began to realize—it was also a very significant one.

Episode 12: An inconsistency and its consequences

Stanley forced himself to spell out his next conclusion very slowly, as if for the benefit of an imaginary Dr Watson. If Eric was writing the cover letter for his manuscript on April 16th then his scribbled PS about Hamblin's sudden return implied Hamblin had come home on that day. But this contradicted Hamblin's own account of finding Eric's body when he got back from Sussex the *following* day—that is, on April 17th. Had Hamblin in fact returned to Bogburgh much sooner than he had told the police? *And if so,* mused Stanley, *what else might follow?*

Perhaps, after his rush to the post box, Eric's manner was still furtive enough to make Hamblin start asking questions. Or maybe Eric simply failed to hide his own copy of the manuscript. But if Hamblin did—no matter how—discover that Eric had secretly completed a new collection then he would surely have been hurt and angry. What if Eric tried walking away from an incipient quarrel? What if Hamblin refused to let things drop and followed him out of the house and toward the nearby cliff top? What if there was an accidental slip (or even a push) leading to a fall?

There were many hypothetical links in the chain of events that Stanley was constructing; but, whatever *did* actually happen at Bogburgh on April 16th, it now seemed probable that Hamblin was more involved in Eric's death than he had ever admitted. And if that were so, it would have made sense for him to write himself out of the tragedy—by first pretending to have come back later than he actually did and then spreading the story of Eric's depression about writer's block. He must have reasoned that this version of events would not be questioned if he deleted the files on Eric's computer and also destroyed (what he thought was) the only copy of the manuscript. He couldn't have known that another copy had already been posted and would, for the next few years, be awaiting discovery in Prince's untidy office. *That package really was a kind of letter bomb*, Stanley thought.

And when, eventually, that bomb went off and Eric's last letter came to light, Prince must surely have put two and two together just as Stanley had done and deduced that Hamblin had been guilty of—at the very least—misleading the police. Did Hamblin's grumpiness and hostility towards his fellow tutor imply that Prince had already told Hamblin of his suspicions? Had Prince even tried to exploit them by, say, offering silence in exchange for a clear run at the McMahon post?

With hindsight Stanley could find evidence to support this blackmail conjecture. It could, for instance, explain the cryptic exchanges accompanying the strange poem-duel between Prince and Hamblin on the first night. And Prince's very deliberate brandishing of Eric's letter in front of Hamblin the previous evening could now be seen as both a taunt and also a warning that disclosure would be very easy.

But wait a minute, Stanley said to himself. *If Prince was using that letter to threaten Hamblin, why did I find it in* Hamblin*'s room?*

The obvious explanation was that Hamblin had somehow managed to get hold of the letter. Prince's provocative gesture would have shown him that it was almost within reach. And that could have suggested the idea of trying to get it back—even by force, since he was the bigger and heavier of the two. So did some sort of confrontation take place in Prince's room late on Wednesday night? If it did and if it turned into a clumsy struggle which left Prince unconscious then Hamblin's childhood memory could supply the very useful idea of staging the roller-towel hanging. If Prince was only knocked out then pressure on his windpipe would soon make a temporary condition permanent. And even if he was already dead the suicide scenario might still be believed.

A mixture of reasoning and guesswork had led Stanley to the conclusion that Hamblin had been responsible for Prince's death. This theory seemed to fit the known facts quite well—but only up to a certain point. What had happened next?

If Hamblin *had* retrieved the incriminating letter he surely had no reason to go back upstairs and kill himself. True, there was a risk of forensic evidence linking him to Prince's death but for the time being he could still have hoped to get away with it.

On the other hand, if Hamblin *didn't* kill himself then Stanley would have to return to his original list of suspects to try and work out who did.

Stanley's further deliberations were interrupted at this point. Mary Maxwell put her head around the door of the library.

Oh, there you are, she said when she saw Stanley. *I wondered where you'd got to. I don't blame you for wandering off; most of our fellow-confinees are scraping the bottoms of their conversational-skills barrels by now!*

Stanley smiled sympathetically and Mary came in and sat down opposite him.

The funny thing is, she said, leaning forward confidentially, *I was once in one of those Agatha Christie-type plays where people are trapped in some remote location and then get murdered one by one. I got despatched in Act Two—poisonous spider, I think. But of course the stage dialogue didn't get stilted and boring—at least it wasn't meant to.* (Here she patted Stanley's hand archly.) *You see we were all supposed to be suspicious of one another; and nobody wanted to be alone in case they became the next victim. But it's not a bit like that here. Nobody's frightened. People are shocked of course but no one feels threatened or even touched.*

Julia seems pretty upset, Stanley said.

Well, yes ... replied Mary thoughtfully. *It's interesting you should mention her. She's not like the rest of us: we didn't really know the three dead people.*

Three? queried Stanley, wondering for a moment if he'd missed something.

Yes. Don't you see? Everything that's happened this week—including the deaths—is centred on Eric. And now Mr Prince and Mr Hamblin are gone there's only Julia who has any connection to him.

Mary paused, as if weighing up how to deliver her next line. *You did understand didn't you that Eric's Nineteen Eighty-Four poem was about Julia? I didn't want to embarrass her—though I did drop a pretty broad hint—but it was obvious to me that she'd always carried a torch for Eric—hopeless of course! That poem was Eric's subtle way of saying he knew and was sorry. Not so subtle actually considering Julia was the name of George Orwell's heroine.*

At the time, Stanley had thought of Mary's response to "Re-reading *Nineteen Eighty-Four*" as overdramatic; but her words now seemed more convincing in view of Julia's earlier behaviour. He told Mary that her theatrical experience must make her rather good at reading people. Mary accepted his compliment gracefully before asking if he'd like to come for a drink since she *absolutely* must *have a large gin to try and make the next hour of this incarceration bearable.*

Stanley wasn't tempted by this invitation. He still had plenty of thinking to do.

Episode 13: A careless mistake

Having politely declined Mary's invitation, Stanley picked up his thoughts where they had been interrupted. He decided however to take a fresh approach. He chose, for the moment, to accept that Hamblin *did* commit suicide, for reasons that were still unclear. The question now arose *Why would he leave a note which was (a) pretty meaningless and (b) an appropriation of his former lover's words?* If he merely wanted to avoid arrest then no note was required. But if he genuinely wanted to explain himself then his chosen method had succeeded only in conveying garbled regrets about his ill-judged behaviour the night before.

Stanley recalled the guests' muddled collective attempt to interpret that cryptic note on Hamblin's door. And then he suddenly realised that there was one person involved in that conversation who *shouldn't* have gone along with the obvious— but incorrect—assumption that the note had actually been written by Hamblin. During the previous night's wrangling about the Jessop manuscript, Prince had pointed out that the covering letter contained an example of Eric's writing and Julia had admitted to recognising it. And yet, only a little while ago, she had talked about the sadness of Hamblin's referring to himself in the third person—*even though she must have known the "suicide note" had not been written by him at all!*

Over the past three days Julia had been a pleasantly efficient background presence, taking care of the needs of the guests. Only lately had her own personality shown itself; and Stanley decided it was time to consider her motives and movements. She had certainly seen Eric's letter before the bottom half was torn off and had perhaps begun to grasp the significance of its scribbled postscript. Her talks with Prince during the week might already have planted the idea that Hamblin knew more about Eric's death than he pretended. Was Julia sitting in her office working out her own theory about Eric's last hours when Hamblin came to ask for help with mopping up spilled whisky?

Stanley reasoned that Hamblin must have come to Julia's office some time after leaving Prince suspended from the roller towel. He would surely have needed a stiff drink at that stage and it would have been unsurprising if he was clumsy when pouring it. (Of course, Hamblin might have staged the accident with the whisky to suggest he'd been drinking alone when Prince met his death: but the truth of Hamblin's story was probably irrelevant to what happened next.)

There were two key questions. Did Julia think Hamblin was, at least partly, to blame for Eric's death? And were her feelings for Eric as deep and lasting as Mary's intuition indicated? If the answers were "yes" then the scene was set for an impulsive act of revenge.

Julia could have added sleeping pills to the triple whisky nightcap she gave Hamblin; or she could have assumed that the drink on its own would knock him out fairly quickly. Either way it would have been easy for her to creep upstairs in the small hours to see if Hamblin was comatose. If he was, then she could slip the bin-bag over his head, tie it securely round his neck and allow him to asphyxiate himself. A few scattered pills would serve as extra set-dressing. But perhaps the note on the door was an improvised embellishment too far.

Stanley reflected that Julia must also have planned further misdirection in order to feign horrified surprise when Hamblin's body was discovered the next day. But in the event her shocked scream at the sight of Prince's body must have been completely genuine since she could not have known about the night's other fatality. After that there would have been no need for her to call on any acting abilities to convey a state of horrified surprise.

Stanley took a deep breath and congratulated himself on devising a plausible solution to the second part of the mystery.

Episode 14: A resolution?

Stanley's explanation of Hamblin's death could now be summarised as a classical revenge story: *J nurses unrequited love for E; J believes H betrayed E; J exacts retribution.* This, along with his equally concise account of Prince's death—*H has a guilty secret; P discovers it; H silences P*—provided a credible solution for both parts of the Weald Barn mystery. But how could he prove it? Should he emulate Sherlock Holmes, the active investigator, or brother Mycroft, the armchair theorist? He could take Eric's letter to the police, tell them his theory and let them look for evidence. Or he could simply give them the letter, with apologies, and keep his conjectures to himself. Then again, he could say nothing at all and leave the police to work with any other circumstantial and forensic evidence they could find.

Stanley didn't think his fellow guests would be able to give the police much help. None of them had seen Eric's letter upon which so much of his case depended. And in any case "self-focussed" was a term that applied pretty well to them all: the pompous and probably sexually frustrated Willoughby; the sentimental and romantic Daisie; the ambitious, mutually absorbed pair Abigail and Barry. Besides himself, only Mary Maxwell seemed to have shown any interest in the other residents of Weald Barn.

By tomorrow afternoon the police would have finished taking statements and all the guests would be free to go their different ways. Abigail and Barry had at least got something to show for their visit in the form of a new relationship (although Stanley doubted it would last very long). Daisie on the other hand would have to go on looking for a life companion. Willoughby would have to go on looking for a publisher (and perhaps for a refund of his workshop fee). Not, Stanley reflected, that he would know the future stories of any of his fellow-guests since he was unlikely to see them again—except perhaps Mary who was bound to turn up on a lunch-time TV soap opera or a late-night re-run of a detective drama.

What Stanley himself had got from his stay at Weald Barn amounted to some unwelcome criticism from Hamblin and an unexpected opportunity for problem solving. He wasn't keen to extend the list of outcomes to include prolonged police interviews and an appearance as a witness in a murder trial. Hence he found himself becoming strongly inclined to quietly destroy and forget the letter he should never have picked up in the first place.

The truth, Stanley had to admit, was that he, like Willoughby, had developed a soft spot for Julia and was not very keen to incriminate her. After all, her (alleged) victim was (probably) a murderer—maybe even a double murderer. And, what's more, he had sneered at Stanley's poetry.

By leaving matters as they stood, Stanley could enjoy all the pleasure of believing he was right—but without going to the trouble of proving it. This pleasant sensation was not one he was permitted to indulge in at his place of work, where he was expected to justify all his mathematical assertions. He had once written a poem recollecting (in tranquility) his wish to prolong the anticipatory glow of conviction which precedes the (possibly frustrating) spadework of formal validation...

BEFORE I PROVED THE THEOREM ...

... I began to write the poem, letting
key assumptions set the rhythm, trying
rhyming schemes for unmade arguments
and dreaming of potential sequences
of riders and corollaries to follow.

At the night time edge of sleep, when freed
from tyrannies of page and pen, conjectures
nimbly shaped themselves as metaphors
whose resonance augmented reasoning
to satisfy blurred versions of equations.

Sums recited in my head suggested
patterns in the DNA of numbers
to explain how primes could propagate
themselves yet keep their pedigree intact
among a throng of mongrel integers.

But eager as I was for QED
I paused before I wrote down each next line
the way seducers tiptoe to the bedroom
via minor step-by-step transgressions,
delightfully yet shrewdly putting off

commitment to explicit proposition—
unambiguous adultery.
For each advance might tread upon an error
like a crumpled rug; and once truth stumbles
she'll remember she must keep her self-respect.

Episode 15: And afterwards...

The statement that Stanley gave the police the next morning contained a minimum of factual information. But it seemed to suffice and he was allowed to go home.

Over the following days the national press gave brief attention to the sudden and unnatural deaths of two well-known poets (although there would probably have been no coverage at all if only *one* poet had been involved). But the story soon disappeared from even the local papers. Obviously it generated more interest within the small world of poetry; but this took the form of speculation and regret rather than serious enquiry. Anyone who now searches media archives for more information will be disappointed. Perhaps an inquest eventually recorded both deaths as suicide. Or perhaps an open verdict was returned because—even though the exact circumstances remained unclear—the police believed no one besides Prince and Hamblin to have been involved.

***

Soon after returning from Weald Barn, Stanley noticed an unwelcome change in his poetry. While solving the mystery he had been able to detach himself from the shock of seeing two not-at-all beautiful corpses. But now his poems all revolved around ugly images of death and his notebook contained such bleak fragments as

> A hangman's hood across its face,
> the heavy head is unsupported
> on a broken neck inside a noose.
> The hangman's ~~hands get wiped~~ wipes his hands upon
> a towel

> I'm imagining a statue
> of a man in anguish ~~standing~~ —Prague
> ~~in a public square;~~ perhaps or Gothenberg
> and words are carved into its plinth
> ~~to prove~~ which state the body's a machine
> designed to measure pain.

> Glancing blows are calibrated
> by their radius of action
> ~~and how fast it shrinks~~
> Aches in cartilage cause less alarm
> than twinges in soft tissue
> like the ~~genitals~~ eyes and genitals.

While Stanley was waiting for his poetic imagination to free itself from these narrow and unpleasant confines, the one surviving paper copy of Eric Jessop's last collection remained in a police storage facility. By now it is probably very deeply buried—and may even be literally buried in a landfill site. So it must, for practical purposes, be regarded as having gone missing yet again. Thus Julia's fear that she would never read Eric Jessop's final poems seemed after all to be well-founded.

***

A couple of years after the ill-starred "Delighting in the Dark Side" workshop, a middle-aged computer enthusiast—who happened also to be an acquaintance of Stanley's—began overhauling an elderly desktop computer he had picked up in a car boot sale. He was intrigued to find the hard disk had deliberately been erased and so he amused himself by trying various tools for recovering the deleted material. He was initially gratified to find he could reconstruct some partially readable files. The content he finally pieced together turned out to be a disappointment, however, when he recognized the enigmatic text as poetry. But because he knew that Stanley had some interest in such stuff he printed out a copy for him.

Out of politeness, Stanley dutifully skimmed through the material and, to his astonishment, he recognized parts of the poem "Re-reading *Nineteen Eighty-Four*". He then realised that fate had entrusted him with the lost Jessop manuscript—or, at least, large parts of it. Once again he found himself in sole possession of important information which he must decide what to do with. To try and publicize his discovery would involve the trouble of proving a connection between Eric Jessop and some files on an old computer. But what else could he do?

The answer, when it came to him, was—in hindsight—an obvious one. After checking that she was still working at Weald Barn (and wondering, in passing, whether workshops had been harder or easier to organise after "Delighting in the Dark Side") Stanley sent Julia the recovered poems along with a note of explanation which concluded *Your extreme loyalty to Eric surely entitles you to custody of his final works. I am content for their existence to remain as another secret we share…*

He did not receive a reply. But he liked to imagine Julia, from time to time, reading and re-reading surviving extracts from "An Image on the Retina"…

An Image on the Retina

ERIC JESSOP

END OF HOLIDAY

So we made a sandcastle.
The tide was out—*and going outer*,
you said—and our *one last swim*
was sucked away. A joyless beach
stretched empty as a London Monday
ninety miles away from you.

To make our sandcastle *just so*
we scrabbled up a loose wide pile
with spades and hands then patted down
the sloping sides and our frustration
with small palms.
                Dry grains slid off
our skin but clung to fine and sun-bleached
forearm hair. Our smoothed-off mound
gained turrets and its drawbridge spanned
a moat that wouldn't fill with water.

You, as usual, started it—
became an aeroplane with arms
for wings; your bombing run took out
one tower with a passing swipe.
Adding sound effects, I followed,
breaching walls while you switched sides
with throat-back, anti-aircraft fire.

We took turns to precision-kick
our fortress to brown sugar-spill
until we both torpedo-flung
our selves full length into the wreck
and wrestled, laughing, limbs entangled,
holding on and holding on.

So? We only made a sandcastle.
Defiance could deflect the blame
for lateness and the state of us.

SAME TIME SOME OTHER YEAR

A cold grey apron of a morning
drapes itself across the beach
where ocean slumps on shingle.
Waves submerge and unsubmerge
long groynes where seagulls launch themselves
in turn like relay swimmers.

A windscreen captures one small patch
of empty sky but does not trap
a stretch of unspent time—
unless those are the same three gulls
repeating mirrored paths between
its unresisting edges.

I'm on my first week and the second
floor in a hotel that's grown
synonymous with yearning.
Maybe Jacqueline is coming—
last year's lithe, swift heroine
of beach and garden games.

Scottie dogs on playing cards
are scattered round my feet, left over
from attempts at patience.
I resent the window glass
that will outlast my tenancy
of these borrowed rooms

where nothing happens but a wish
to be outside. Kit Carson's waiting,
hidden in the bushes:
if I get there first he'll choose me
for his cricket team; or let me
sit with her at lunch.

Teenage boys drag two canoes
across wet pebbles, undiscouraged
by another re-launch.
A notice board is wind-and-sanded
to a blank so they must guess
all risks from tides or currents.

Unkeeled memories capsize
as easily as boats: retrieval
is not trivial
down there among tall breakers—taller
than an eight-year-old entranced
by Jacqueline's black swimsuit.

SLOW TURNS OF EVENTS (1)

An oceanographer, off duty
on a Hebridean holiday,
misreads the tides ahead of going swimming—
thereby going missing.

A hungry ornithologist
observes it's time somebody wrote
a brand-new *Guide to British Birds
and How to Cook Them.*

A windswept vicar on the Lleyn
peninsula believes his cure of souls
includes the birds. His bishop calls him
RSPB Thomas.

ASCENDING

It's an April day
that could go either way
to sun or showers
and so could we
between the village
(food and shelter)
and the ruins
(the some-still-standing stones
whose legend fetched us here)

The lark surprises us
doing what (you knew)
all larks will do
and climbing to a place
of commentary
lyrically mimicking
my incredulity
and ecstasy
that you and I have come this far

We might pretend
its notes were tokens
of encouragement
for us to press ahead

(finding no significance
in the sudden plunge
when the song was finished)

SIMMER GENTLY

We peeled each other with long strokes
of sharpened silence,
knowing well enough, without salt water,
whatever we exposed would go an ugly black.

Then, side by side, we sliced the evidence.
While I was shredding it to almost-pulp
you were slashing quickly criss-cross
to dismissive squares
that kept a ruined semblance of whole fruit.

    The need to eat diverted us
    and made a menu neutral ground
    to meet on briefly.
    Each remembered, privately,
    how choosing food together used to feel
    like making one more small commitment—
    before, that is, we'd ever thought
    betrayals could occur.

When we came back, ingredients
were spread across the table
needing to be blended
but the recipe was missing.

Which left it up to both of us
to taste and test
if hints of a suspicion were sufficient
or if what was wanted was a pinch of salt.

EN SUITE

The soap lies sticky on its bed of stones.
Above the coral-coloured basin,
where I'm slowly working lather
round my fingers, there's a recessed mirror:
it reflects a bedroom with a pair of towels
tossed across a counterpane.

Small brushes, creams and lip-gloss hint
at semi-private body-care
artlessly exposed. Though fully dressed,
I'm sensing someone else's nakedness
is commonplace in here. A musky tang
of perfume drifts in from a garden
where children's voices rise and fall.

Early evening sunlight penetrates
the frosted window, making sparkle points
on vertices of cut-glass bottles
twinkling as distractingly
as mind's-eye-catching fantasies
I'd hesitate to own out loud.

WARNING OFF

The image of your bright hooped shirt,
silky like a jockey's colours,
is riding rings around my heart.

He's always had a soft spot for me
you confide, *and now I've told him
why it couldn't work.* I'm glad,
poor sod, and sorry for him too;
for sitting near you day on day
must make it hard to hide devotion.

You keep cool and gracious: patient
with his pestering, you'll meet him
sometimes where you feel you can
and smile to tell him when you can't.

He's hoping I might change my mind.
Again, poor sod: your gentleness
is worked inside his head to something
else on nights like this when weary
words reshape themselves to form
a well-worn, wanted phrase or saying—

just as I know I'll replay
this conversation and convince
myself it really did conceal
no coded messages for me.

SLOW TURNS OF EVENTS (2)

An orthopaedic surgeon knows smashed bones
will mend—and stronger than before.
As a kindness to his patient
he breaks the other one.

When accused, a judge suspects his wife
will disbelieve denials so confesses
falsely. He then finds forgiveness
takes a full three months.

An empress, favouring her son
to hide the unmaternal fact
she doesn't like him much, betrays the daughter
whom she truly loves.

MAYBE NOT

When time and photo-chemicals
of memory combine, they seldom fix
a picture sharp and shaded as those dreams
you wake from sad, impossibly
intent on scrambling back to them

the way you tumbled through that passage
from the January riverside
into a narrow dark-oak pub
and settled by a failing fire
into a self-absorbing conversation
with a girl about a slim blue book.

She interrupted, telling you
another man was driving her
to strive for championship form
at volleyball in four years' time.

But don't you wish, you interrupted back,
*that someone else instead would run
his hands along your hips and draw
you lower more than lift you higher?*

Maybe not, she answered, growing
boyishly attractive, *though
I fully understand the offer
is well-meant.* The slim blue book
contained bilingual—Welsh and English—
model letters, starting with
a short, regretful note rejecting
an older gentleman's proposal.

TWO MINUTES' SILENCE

Cyrillic writing comes as a surprise
beside a cliff top church in Ceredigion.
Beneath the name, the monument explains
itself in Welsh: *merch Rwsiaidd*—
a Russian girl, washed overboard, you guess,
unmissed until her passing ship had passed.

Or did somebody stretcher her ashore?
The stone says 1936: perhaps
she was a runaway who'd smuggled sickness
with her self out of a homeland that she feared
would grudge her even earth for burial?

Her grave is flowerless among
the better-visited memorials
to Owen, Rhys and Morgan. So you pause
and lay your curiosity
in place of missing wreaths and leave
its fading scent of good intentions.

Above her body, now as fleshless
as an unshared, unembroidered story,
your stiff invisible bouquet ensures
the Russian girl remains a little longer
just this side of unforgotten.

MOURNERS

Their first funeral. Two children
won't expect to see their parents,
later, chuckling over scotch
or unaccustomed sweetish sherry.

On the evening of the day
he's seen his father die, a husband
shocks his wife by coming home
in his Dad's old pullover.

A stay-home daughter hears (ghost) footsteps
in (empty) bedrooms overhead;
she does and doesn't want the phantom
to descend the (actual) stairs.

Beside the hearse, a sudden widow,
unprepared for utter change,
counterfeits a smiling face
to soothe an anxious grandchild's fears.

A widower's concealed distress
was less for what was lost than what
he stalked for years and kept pretending
not to know he'd never have.

FEELING THE COLD

Whatever may be true, I'm sure
enough to tell myself
I'm treading where my forebears used to
trudge across hard fields
toward the sandstone certainty of church
to huddle in a winter congregation,
pinch-faced and jostling like penned cattle.

I guess the chancel's barely changed.
Dust drifts among the sallow smells
of wood and wax. It carries memories
and remnants of their breath
to mix invisibly with mine.

Snow and gospel, visiting again,
disguised as new arrivals,
hide the graveyard's hardened scars
and dress its half-healed wounds.

Sharp cold's a pain that's eased
by stamping feet and fire
and meat and ale and company
when squire and parson sanction them.

Blunt grief must make do
with less substantial consolations:
a father's hasty, muddled blessing
muttered in a husky voice
with a hand laid on the shoulder
of a rough-made coffin.

ADAGIO

The last log's glow subsides. It's time
to bundle blankets on this borrowed sofa
and unplug the Christmas tree.
Beyond thin curtains
cold slides down outside the window

where tattered mist an hour ago
moved up the path ahead of us
to drape the trees and blend with woodsmoke
into incense for the secular,
augmenting shreds of choral anthem

clinging to us since those closing echoes
hovered over vestry chatter
and big plates of fruit cake for small boys
who swapped white robes for anoraks
to lead us over midnight water meadows.

A make-do bed; a tree already shedding
needles; drifting smoke and chilly mist
unzipping breath; those ringing wineglass voices
that must break: it's still a mystery
the way in which these things all hold together.

SLOW TURNS OF EVENTS (3)

A priest gets called a leveller
for stirring up his congregation
to insurgence. He ends up horizontal,
a shepherd trampled by his flock.

Two reluctant executioners
are persuaded they should take the job
so they can kill with greater kindness
than more eager applicants.

A soldier and a surgeon
between them steal a poet's larynx;
to give his verse a voice again he needs
the skills of a ventriloquist.

URBAN CONCEALMENT

After "Le città invisibili" by Italo Calvino

The city is reticent about its past.
The not-so-well-remembered layers:
fallen walls, worn floors,
smashed grave- and paving-stones,
stay folded like a gambler's cards—
private even as the lifelines
on the gambler's hand.

The present fills the gaps in pencil strokes:
the horizontal lintels over doorways;
the verticals of lightning rods
and empty flagpoles.
Criss-cross window grills are shadow-doubled
onto kitchen whitewash;
banister diagonals
smooth the sawtooth of a staircase
to a long descending slide.

Though the city does not speak
its surfaces display graffiti tags,
as meaningless as punctuation
in a rubbed-out sentence.
The cemetery wall supports a love note
to the local football team;
sprayed paint by a dried-up fountain
announces *You can't stop the sun
with a policeman's gun.*

The city is reticent about its past.
Too-many-to-remember layers
of betrayals, failed alliances
and deals unrealised are locked
in legal boxes and confessionals—
or else denied as utterly
as an unmarked grave.

FREE RUNNING

> *Then the Lord called to the man clothed in linen who had the writing kit "Go through the city and put a mark on the foreheads of those who lament over all the detestable things that are done in it."*
> — Ezekiel 9

Here's a runner in a linen loin cloth,
tight-corked inkwell swinging from his belt.
His sandalled feet go padding over paving
stones along triumphal avenues
or skid on straw and faeces in dark alleys.

His stylus doubles as a baton, passed
between the dozens like him, checking scores
of zig-zag streets—perhaps near you? Yet mostly
he's ignored: he's no Olympic torch-man,
cheered on through a smug metropolis.

Evidently grieving's what you do
to gain exemption from whatever vengeance
he's predicting for your city's misdeeds.
Better shed real tears, then: don't assume
self-righteous grumbling gets you any marks.

STREET THEATRE

> *Then lie down on your left side, and I will place on you the guilt of Israel. When you finish that, turn over on your right side and suffer for the guilt of Judah. I will tie you up so that you cannot turn from one side to the other.*
> — Ezekiel 4

He wonders why his precious flesh remains
unbruised beside the gutters of the Barbican
where he's laid himself down and kept
extended silence. He remembers sighing
when he acquiesced to wearing shackles
as a wider warning of impending
penalties implicit in black axioms
hidden in the pockets of dark suits
on busy men who step around him.

Amid the mud he is meticulous
to promise no more than he knows
and threaten nothing less. Yet ten times more
ignore him than will meet his eyes
or scan his dumb-show doomsday tokens.
No shift in his position is permitted
to trip up passers-by and overturn
their bland indifference to sewage stink
of wet corruption clinging to their ankles.
He marvels that his holy bones
still hold together in his fragile carcase.

SICK IN A STRANGE CITY

A common condition

Your body has reneged on obligations
you took lightly—till they were ungranted.
Sumps to drain discomfort are all clogged
and levels in a worry-reservoir
surge around uneasy medium.

Unmanned and far away from your familiar
surroundings, you are suddenly and randomly
at one with anyone who's lost.
                            Magnetic north
can't move, but anybody's compass can be biased
by a load of iron stuffed into his knapsack.
Needles swing toward immediacy of need:
addiction fixes on its fix and hunger trumps
taboos on scavenging. Surrendering to bullies
may defer a beating: but it's worth a fight,
when homeless, to secure a rank abandoned mattress.

Now you'll gladly pay a walk-in clinic
anything to fix up your malfunction.

A feverish reaction

Waiting on the clinic's plastic chairs
for your collusion are old newspapers.
They tempt you into turning over scraps
of someone else's suffering to spread
their anguish even further, like infection.

A taxi-driver clumsily attacked—
for money, not his life—becomes a body
undiscovered in the trunk for days
while agencies ignore his room-mate's phone calls.

Defeated beauty, bedbound, locks her door,
refusing carers; untouched lunch congeals
beside a nearly empty whisky bottle.

Thirteen-year-old discontent has yearned
for sixteen's fancied glamour and begins
a willing spiral into victimhood.
In darkened parking lots below the mall
inadequate but cunning kidnappers
pretend their promises of fashion-shoots.
Police take morning-mist soft-focus pictures
on a golf-course in the deepest rough.

Awaiting diagnosis

Your test results will soon come back. A television
in one corner of the room live-screens the ending
of a siege with shots outside a half-burned house.
A leather jacket, draped, half-hides a hopeless face.

You imagine guilt, when cornered, smells like fear
of being taken to a room without an exit
to be blamed. A dandruff-shabby lawyer offers
token bored advice, suggests a guilty plea
to lesser charges as a way of carpeting
the corridor that leads in any case to blows
and scalding in the showers—all for something petty
when it happened.
    When it happened, primitive
reaction was too easily mistaken for
a genuine imperative: let's make it better
now and brandish jagged panic or drive faster
into roadblocks built with slabs of bad decisions.

Treatment & discharge

With symptoms muted by a box of pills,
you're going home where prospects of a doctor's
probing latex glove seem less invasive.

Escape commences in a station entrance.
where local casual anger hangs around
with gangs of greasy leather jackets, curl-peaked
baseball caps. Its short infrequent words,
while still unsaid, are shaped by brutal squares
of thinly razored-down moustache and beard.
Its hand, unoccupied by beer, propels
a hard black rubber ball again, again
against a step to catch it bouncing back
erratically, as if dodging logic.

From your paid-for window seat you watch
the trackside cables dip and rise to nod
in reassurance you'll be getting back
the rights the world's already granted you
to make smart choices.
     If you lose your glasses
you'll decipher rules and prices badly:
but whatever you half-see you can
half-guess and half-remember what it means
and what you have to do.
     If some can't read
then what they never knew, they'll never know.

SLOW TURNS OF EVENTS (4)

The man who prints bad news
about the government has vanished
like his predecessors. Absent headlines
tell his story for him.

Three clowns, dowsing, stumble
on a spring of laughter—which gets blocked
when each one tries diverting it
to his own private joke.

A self-taught songsmith
cannot transcribe music so he hums
melodies to an amanuensis
sprawled beside him in the bath.

DAWN SOLO

When he used to play the music-halls
he'd pseudo-rhapsodise about the joys
of waking up on smoggy Hackney mornings
list'nin' to the sparrers cough be'ind the gasworks.

Now, getting up at 4 a.m.
to let some air into the bedroom
he inadvertently admits a clutch of notes
like pebbles tossed against a window
or coins thrown in a busker's cup:

a stuttered burst of birdsong,
repeated like a loop of tape,
his young friend Eric maybe could identify
although the sound is partly drowned
by the whistling breathing of his partner
and the clack of someone's suitcase wheels
heading for an early morning flight.

A solitary chorister
is doing what his species is supposed to:
claiming and defending territory—but
against imaginary challengers.
Blame diesel fumes, the neighbours' cats,
the urban foxes if you like. The fact is this:
the only other feathers in this street are pigeons'.

The gasworks and their smokestack have all gone
and nah there ain't no sparrers rahnd 'ere eiver.
He finds he can't remember if he ever knew
whether they could sing or not.

DOUBLE ENTRY

I scrawl alternate lines in red and black
in jottings from my cottage window seat:
a frosted flock of sheep queues down the track
in search of grass that's thawed enough to eat.

Bored cashiers in nineteen-fifties banks
might scratch alternate lines in red and black
to make accounting matters seem like pranks
on customers. The queue sprawls round the back.

We're shoved behind our windows without lunch
the cashiers whine inside their thrifty bank
until the books all balance. Then the branch
can talk of country matters for a prank.

A clock strikes, curt, abrupt as thin-sliced bread.
I should be buying sandwiches for lunch
but won't step out on unsure-footed tread
if rooks can't balance on an icy branch.

This staircase shows me I'm as past my prime
as dry and curling crusts of thin-sliced bread;
I'm sidling, as if spirals were a crime,
to venture unsure-footed down each tread.

The draining bathtub gulps and chokes and gags
as if on stale cake served well past its prime;
hair, froth and skin flakes go down like old lags
sliding in a spiral back to crime.

We keep facts logged: it's myths we hear played back.
Time grinds our truths to pulp—no jokes or gags—
and guzzles what was us: a little track
of froth, like snowflake ghosts, is all that lags

Our stepped-on memories, like creaking planks,
wake sleeping dogs who, with their ears laid back,
herd us to pens. Before we've said *no thanks*
projectionists pick films from long grey racks
and screen our troubled lives in reds and blacks.

WHEN THE PHOTOGRAPH WAS TAKEN

.... he was almost out of shot
and standing in that other room,
whose shelves were packed with almanacs.
He clasped a chair back in both hands
while staring through the leaded window.
Snow was melting down the glass
but clung to kinks in twigs, like sherbet
scooped from pre-war paper bags
in the crooks of small boys' fingers.

... the women wore bright summer frocks
yet it was wintry where he stood
and gripped the chair with shoulders shrugged
in very far from unconcern.
His back was hunched against a cold
refusing to explain itself.
Frost and mist had turned the house
across the road to black and white—
a mirror-image *doppelganger*
mockery of home from home.

... he was drawing breath to tell
a story, waiting for his opening
sentences to come along
the gravel path between the graveyard
and the hospital, like parcels
in a Christmas postman's sack.
And while his back was turned he missed
the story of their failed attempt
to prove he wasn't even there
when the photograph was taken.

AN IMAGE ON THE RETINA

The bull collapses, forelegs buckling
at the second poleaxe blow.
Its eyeballs freeze two cameo reflections
of the slaughterman, bare-lit
beside a smeared and spattered wall.
But does its retina retain a pinhole
replica of abattoir and butcher?

Biologists once thought they might retrieve
such latent images as indisputable
eye-witness evidence in murder trials.
They demand no effort on the victim's part

whereas the hired assassin must take pains
to memorize a snapshot likeness then locate
their quarry in a crowd—as salesmen learn
to spot a prospect they can fix their sights on.

And prophets, similarly focussed, smugly claim
they always keep their eyes upon the future, knowing
most of us look back too often at ourselves
mirrored in opinions and shop windows.

If our mirrors soaked up what they saw
then, when one breaks, the trapped reflections
would come tumbling like a roughly shuffled deck
of fortune-teller's cards to spill the past
instead of spelling out the future.

Accumulated hindsight stacks up accusations—
not about our latest wrongs so much
as what we could have been and weren't. Reflected truth
might show us we were always beautiful
and lovable. And that we've wasted both.